Best Garden Plants for New Jersey

Lorraine Kiefer • *Alison Beck*

Lone Pine Publishing International

The Distributor: Lone Pine Publishing
1808 B Street NW, Suite 140
Auburn, WA, USA 98001
Website: www.lonepinepublishing.com

Library and Archives Canada Cataloguing in Publication

Library and Archives Canada Cataloguing in Publication

Kiefer, Lorraine, 1944-
   Best garden plants for New Jersey / Lorraine Kiefer, Alison Beck.

Includes index.
ISBN-13: 978-976-8200-31-0

   1. Plants, Ornamental—New Jersey. 2. Gardening—New Jersey.
I. Beck, Alison, 1971- II. Title.

SB453.2.N5K53 2007   635.909749   C2006-906782-1

Front cover photographs by Tamara Eder except where noted (clockwise from top right): Pat Austin rose, daylily (Tim Matheson), daylily, lilac foliage, daylily (Tim Matheson), lily (Laura Peters), columbine, lily (Erika Flatt), flowering cherry.

All photos by Tamara Eder, Tim Matheson and Laura Peters except: AASelection 24a; Janet Davis 70b; Joan de Grey 130b; Therese D'Monte 132b; Erv Evans-NCSU 95a; Derek Fell 47a, 58a, 70a, 88a, 95b, 103a, 104a, 105a&b, 109, 128b, 129a, 143, 149b; Erika Flatt 82a, 126b, 131a, 163a; Anne Gordon 62, 133b; Lynne Harrison 94a&b; Saxon Holt 47b, 104b, 133a, 149a; Duncan Kelbaugh 126a; Lorraine Kiefer 9b; Liz Klose 165a, 167a&b; Debra Knapke 135a; Dawn Loewen 57a, 83a; Janet Loughrey 55b, 74a, 132a, 156a; Marilynn McAra 130a; Kim O'Leary 11b, 64a, 66a&b, 85b, 115b; Allison Penko 44a, 50a, 77a, 81b, 84b, 92a&b, 100b, 116b, 118a, 121b, 151a, 152a, 154a, 161a, 162b, 165b, 166b; Photos.com 128a, 134a; Robert Ritchie 37b, 39a, 42a, 65b, 90a, 102a, 110a, 119a, 144a; Leila Sidi 134b; Star Roses 103b, 111, 112; Peter Thompstone 20a, 45a, 52b; Mark Turner 55a, 58b, 59a&b, 72a, 74b, 86a&b 97a, 117, 129b; Don Williamson 119b, 125b, 127a&b, 135b, 137a; Tim Wood 65a, 73a, 101a.

PC: P13

Table of Contents

Introduction

Starting a garden can seem like a daunting task, but is also an exciting and rewarding adventure. With so many plants to choose from, the challenge is deciding which ones and how many to include in your garden. This book is intended to give beginning gardeners the information they need to start planning and planting gardens of their own. It describes a wide variety of plants and provides basic descriptions of plants, planting and growing information and tips for use, all to help create a beautiful and functional landscape.

New Jersey is known as the Garden State with good reason. We have one of the most wonderful climates in the entire world. We can boast of four distinct seasons that combine the best of north and south, with extremes generally falling between 0° and 100° F. Missing are the extended deep freezes of the north and the oppressive heat of the south. While the extremes of north and south are possible in New Jersey, they are generally short in duration, never lasting more than a few weeks. The climate of New Jersey is varied with ample rainfall and summer heat, both of which are good for growing plants and crops.

New Jersey also has a varied landscape. The coastal area has a light, sandy soil that is usually acidic. There are many rolling hills and flat areas that have a wonderful garden loam that is good for agriculture. In the northernmost corner of the state there are mountains with a diverse list of native plants. Found in a pocket in the southern and central area of the state near the coast, the Pine Barrens are a unique area with such diverse flora that botanists from all over come to see the plants that grow in the sandy, sterile, acidic soil. Water is plentiful throughout the state, with a large network of streams and rivers running toward the sea.

Hardiness zones and frost dates are two terms often used when discussing climate and gardening. USDA hardiness zones are based on the minimum possible winter temperatures. Plants are rated based on the zones in which they grow successfully. The last frost date in spring combined with the first frost date in fall allows us to predict the length of the growing season and gives us an idea of when we can begin planting out in spring. In New Jersey, zones range from zone 5b or 6a in the northern regions, with winter temperatures as low as -15° F, to the southern coastal areas considered by some to be as mild as USDA zone 8a, where temperatures generally never go below 0° F. The largest part of New Jersey is generally a USDA zone 6 or 7, with variable temperatures typical of the Middle Atlantic States.

Microclimates are small areas that are generally warmer or colder than the surrounding area. Buildings, fences, trees and other large structures can provide extra shelter in winter but may trap heat in summer, thus creating a warmer microclimate. The bottoms of hills are usually colder than the tops, but may not be as windy. Take advantage of these areas when you plan your garden and choose your plants; you may even grow out-of-zone plants successfully in a warm, sheltered location.

Getting Started

When planning your garden, start with a quick analysis of the garden as it is now. Plants have different requirements, and it is best to put the right plant in the right place rather than to try and change your garden to suit the plants you want.

Knowing which parts of your garden receive the most and least amounts of sunlight will help you choose the proper plants and decide where to plant them. Light is classified into four basic groups: full sun (direct, unobstructed light all or most of the day); partial shade (direct sun for about half the day and shade for the rest); light shade (shade all or most of the day with some sun filtering through to ground level); and full shade (no direct sunlight). Most plants prefer a certain amount of light, but many can adapt to a range of light levels.

Soil is the foundation of a good garden. Plants use soil to hold themselves upright, and they also rely on the many resources it holds: air, water, nutrients, organic matter and a host of microbes. The particle size of the soil influences the amount of air, water and nutrients it can hold. Sand, with the largest particles, has lots of air space but allows water and nutrients

Hardiness Zones Map

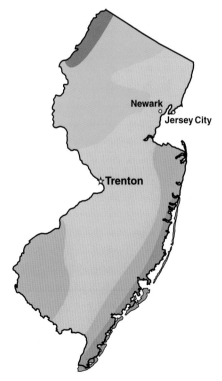

Newark

Jersey City

Trenton

Average Annual Minimum Temperature	
5b	-15 to -10
6a	-10 to -5
6b	-5 to 0
7a	0 to 5
7b	5 to 10

to drain quickly. Clay, with the smallest particles, is high in nutrients but has very little air space. Water is therefore slow to penetrate clay and slow to drain from it.

Soil acidity or alkalinity (measured on the pH scale) influences the amount and type of nutrients available to plants. A pH of 7 is neutral; a lower pH is more acidic. Most plants prefer soil with a pH of 5.5–7.5. Soil testing kits are available at most garden centers, and soil samples can be sent to testing facilities for a more thorough analysis. This will give you an idea of what plants will do well in your soil, and what amendments might need to be made to your soil.

Compost is one of the best and most important amendments you can add to any type of soil. Compost improves soil by adding organic matter and nutrients, introducing soil microbes, increasing water retention and improving drainage. You can purchase compost, or you can make it in your own backyard.

Selecting Plants
It's important to purchase healthy plants that are free of pests and diseases. Such plants will establish quickly in your garden and won't introduce problems that may spread to other plants. You should have a good idea of what the plant is supposed to look like—the color and shape of the leaves and the habit of the plant—and then inspect the plant for signs of disease or insect damage.

The majority of plants are started in containers. This is an efficient way for nurseries and greenhouses to grow plants, but when plants grow in a restricted space for too long, they can become pot bound, with their roots densely encircling the inside of the pot. Avoid purchasing plants in this condition; they are often stressed and can take longer to establish. It is often possible to remove pots temporarily to look at the condition of the roots. You can check for soil-borne insects, rotten roots and girdling or pot-bound roots all at the same time. If you do purchsse pot-bound plants, the roots must be lightly pruned or teased apart before planting.

Planting Basics
The following tips apply to all plants.

• Prepare the garden before planting. Remove weeds, make any needed amendments and dig or till the soil in preparation for planting if you are starting a new landscape. If you want to add a single plant to an established bed, you'll have to work around the other plants. The prepared area should be the size of the plant's mature root system.

• Know the mature size. Position plants based on how big they will grow rather than how big they are when you plant them. Large plants should have enough room to mature without interfering with walls, roof overhangs, power lines, walkways or surrounding plants.

Gently remove container.

Ensure proper planting depth.

Backfill with soil.

- Accommodate the root ball. If you prepared your planting spot ahead of time to accommodate the mature roots, your planting hole will only need to be big enough to accommodate the root ball with the roots spread out slightly.

- Unwrap the roots. It is always best to remove any container before planting to give roots the chance to spread out naturally when planted. In particular, you should remove plastic containers, fiber pots and wire. Fiber pots decompose very slowly, if at all, and wick moisture away from the plant. The only exceptions to this rule are the peat pots, pellets and natural burlap; these decompose and can be planted with the young transplants. Peat pots should be sliced down the sides and any of the pot that will be exposed aboveground removed to prevent water from being wicked away from the roots. Burlap should be unwrapped from the trunk and pulled away from the top of the root ball once it is positioned in the planting hole.

- Plant at the same depth. Plants generally like to grow at a certain level in relation to the soil and should be planted at the same level they were at in the pot or container before you transplanted them.

- Settle the soil with water. Good contact between the roots and the soil is important, but if you press the soil down too firmly, as often happens when you step on the soil, you can cause compaction, which reduces the movement of water through the soil and leaves very few air spaces. Instead, pour water in as you fill the hole with soil. The water will settle the soil evenly without allowing it to compact.

- Water deeply. It's better to water deeply once every week or two, depending on the plant, rather than water a little bit more often. Deep and thorough watering forces roots to grow as they search for water and helps them survive dry spells when water bans may restrict your watering regime. Always check the root zone before you water, as some soils hold more water longer than other soils. Over watering can occur when gardeners depend on automatic lawn irrigation and don't check the soil first. Mulching helps retain moisture and reduces watering needs. Containers are the watering exception; they can quickly dry out and may even need watering every day.

- Identify your plants. Keep track of what's what in your garden by putting a tag next to each plant when you plant it. A gardening journal is also a great place to list the plants you have and where you planted them. It is very easy for beginning and seasoned gardeners alike to forget exactly what they planted and where they planted it.

Settle backfilled soil with water.

Water the plant well.

Add a layer of mulch.

Choosing plants

When choosing the plants, you want try to aim for a variety of sizes, shapes, textures, features and bloom times. Features like decorative fruit, variegated or colorful leaves and interesting bark provide interest when plants aren't blooming. This way you will have a garden that captivates your attention all year.

Annuals

Annuals are planted new each year and are only expected to last for a single growing season. Their flowers and decorative foliage provide bright splashes of color and can fill in spaces around immature trees, shrubs and perennials.

Annuals are easy to plant and are usually sold in small cell-packs of four or six. The roots quickly fill the space in these packs, so the root ball should be broken up before planting. I often split the ball in two up the center or run my thumb up each side to break up the roots.

Many annuals are grown from seed and can be started directly in the garden once the soil begins to warm up.

Perennials

Perennials grow for three or more years. They usually die back to the ground each fall and send up new shoots in spring, though they can also be evergreen or semi-shrubby. They often have a shorter period of bloom than annuals, but they require less care.

Many perennials benefit from being divided every few years, usually in early spring while plants are still dormant or, in some cases, after flowering. This keeps them growing and blooming vigorously, and in some cases controls their spread. Dividing involves digging the plant up, removing dead debris, breaking the plant into several pieces using a sharp knife, spade or saw and replanting some or all of the pieces. Extra pieces can be shared with family, friends and neighbors.

Trees & Shrubs

Trees and shrubs provide the bones of the garden. They are often the slowest growing plants, but usually live the longest. Characterized by leaf type, they may be deciduous or evergreen and needled or broad-leaved.

Trees should have as little disturbed soil as possible at the bottom of the planting hole. Loose dirt settles over time, and sinking even an inch can kill some trees. The prepared area for trees and shrubs needs to be at least two to four times bigger than the root ball.

Staking, sometimes recommended for newly planted trees, is only necessary for trees over 5' tall. Stakes support the root ball until it grows enough to support the tree. Stakes should allow the trunk to move with the wind.

Pruning is more often required for shrubs than trees. It helps them maintain an attractive shape and can improve blooming.

Trees and shrubs provide backbone to the mixed border.

Roses are lovely on their own or in mixed borders.

Lilies provide wonderful color and form.

Roses

Roses are beautiful shrubs with lovely, often fragrant blooms. Traditionally, most roses only bloomed once in the growing season, but new varieties bloom all, or almost all, summer. Recurrent or repeat-blooming roses should be dead-headed to encourage more flower production. One-time bloomers should be left for the colorful hips that develop.

Most roses prefer a fertile, well-prepared planting area. A rule of thumb is to prepare an area 24" across, front to back and side to side, and 24" deep. Add plenty of compost or other fertile organic matter and keep roses well watered during the growing season. Many roses are quite durable and will adapt to poorer conditions. Grafted roses should be planted with the graft two inches below the soil line. When watering, avoid getting water on the foliage to reduce the spread of black spot.

Vines

Vines or climbing plants are useful for screening and shade, especially in a location too small for a tree. They may be woody or herbaceous and annual or perennial. Vines either physically cling to surfaces, have wrapping tendrils or stems or need to be tied in place with string.

Sturdy trellises, arbors, porch railings, fences, walls, poles and trees are all possible vine supports. If a support is needed, ensure it's in place before you plant to avoid disturbing the roots later. Choose a support that is suitable for the vine you are growing. It needs to be sturdy enough to hold the plant up and should match the growing habit—clinging, wrapping or tied—of the vine.

Bulbs, Corms & Tubers

These plants have fleshy underground storage organs that allow them to survive extended periods of dormancy. They are often grown for the bright splashes of color their flowers provide in either spring, summer or fall. Each has an ideal depth and time of year at which it should be planted.

Hardy bulbs can be left in the ground and will flower every year. Some popular tender plants are grown from bulbs, corms or tubers and are generally lifted from the garden in late summer or fall as

Many herbs grow well in pots.

the foliage dies back. These are stored in a cool, frost-free location for winter and are replanted in spring.

Herbs

Herbs are plants with medicinal, culinary or other economic purposes. A few common culinary herbs are included in this book. Even if you don't cook with them, the often-fragrant foliage adds its aroma to the garden, and the plants can be quite decorative in form, leaf and flower.

Ornamental grasses add color, variety and texture.

A conveniently placed container—perhaps near the kitchen door—of your favorite herbs will yield plenty of flavor and fragrance all summer.

Many herbs have pollen-producing flowers that attract butterflies, bees, hummingbirds and predatory insects to your garden. Predatory insects feast on problem insects such as aphids, mealy bugs and whiteflies.

Ferns, Grasses & Groundcovers

Many plants are grown for their decorative foliage rather than their flowers, which may also be decorative. Some of these are included in other sections of this book, but we have set aside a few for the unique touch their foliage adds to the garden. Ornamental grasses, ferns, groundcovers and other foliage plants add a variety of colors, textures and forms to the garden.

Ornamental grasses and grass-like plants provide interest all year when the withered blades are left to stand all winter. They are cut back in early spring and divided when the clumps begin to die out in the center.

Ferns provide a lacy foliage accent and combine attractively with broad-leaved perennials and shrubs. Although some ferns will survive in full sun, they are a much more common sight in moist and shady gardens.

A Final Comment

The more you discover about the fascinating world of plants, whether from books, other gardeners and their designs or experimenting with something new in your own garden, the more rewarding your gardening experience will be. This book is intended as a guide to germinate and grow your passion for plants.

Begonia
Begonia

Begonias have beautiful flowers, a compact habit and decorative foliage; there is sure to be one to fulfill your shade gardening needs.

Growing

Begonias prefer **light shade** or **partial shade**, though some wax begonias tolerate sun if their soil is kept moist. The soil should be **fertile, rich in organic matter, well drained** and **neutral to acidic**. Allow the soil to dry out slightly between watering, particularly for tuberous begonias. Begonias love warm weather, so don't plant them before the soil warms in spring. If they sit in cold soil, they may become stunted and fail to thrive. Cuttings are very easy to make if you want to propagate a favorite plant.

Tips

All begonias are useful for shaded garden beds and planters. The trailing tuberous varieties can be used in hanging baskets and along rock walls where the flowers will cascade over the edges. Wax begonias have a neat, rounded habit that makes them particularly attractive as edging plants. Rex begonias, with their dramatic foliage, are useful as specimen plants in containers and beds.

Recommended

B. Rex Cultorum hybrids (rex begonias) are grown for their dramatic, colorful foliage. They should be grown in pots and then brought indoors in winter.

B. semperflorens (wax begonias) have pink, white, red or bicolored flowers and green, bronze, reddish or white variegated foliage.

B. Rex Cultorum hybrids 'Escargot' (above)
B. semperflorens (below)

B. x tuberhybrida (tuberous begonias) are generally sold as tubers and are popular for their flowers that grow in many shades of red, pink, yellow, orange or white. They can be grown inside by a window in winter.

Features: pink, white, red, yellow, orange, bicolored or picotee flowers; decorative foliage
Height: 6–24" **Spread:** 6–24"

Calendula
Calendula

C. officinalis 'Apricot Surprise' (above)
C. officinalis (below)

Calendulas are bright and charming, producing attractive flowers in warm colors from late spring to early summer and again in fall.

Calendula flowers are popular kitchen herbs that can be added to stews for color or salads for flavoring. They can also be brewed into an infusion that is useful as a wash for minor cuts and bruises.

Growing

Calendulas do equally well in **full sun** or **partial shade**. They like cool weather and can withstand a moderate frost. The soil should be of **average fertility** and **well drained**. Deadhead to prolong blooming and to keep the plants looking neat. If they fade in summer heat, cut them back to 4–6" above the ground to promote new growth, or pull them up and seed new ones. Either method will provide a good fall display. Most will self-sow, but sow seed directly into the garden in early spring.

Tips

This informal plant looks attractive in a border, an herb garden or a vegetable patch. It can also be used in planters. Calendula is a cold-hardy annual and often continues flowering, even through a layer of snow, until the ground freezes completely.

Recommended

C. officinalis is a vigorous, tough, upright plant that bears daisy-like, single or double flowers in a wide range of yellow and orange shades. Several cultivars are available.

Also called: pot marigold, English marigold
Features: cream, yellow, gold, orange or apricot flowers; long blooming period
Height: 10–24" **Spread:** 8–20"

Cleome

Cleome

Create a bold and exotic display in your garden with these lovely and unusual flowers that are sure to attract butterflies and hummingbirds.

Growing

Cleomes prefer **full sun** but tolerate partial shade. These plants adapt to most soils, though mixing in organic matter to help retain water is a good idea. Cleomes are drought tolerant but perform best when watered regularly. Pinch out the tip of the center stem on young plants to encourage branching and more blooms. Deadhead plants early in the season to prolong blooming and to reduce prolific self-seeding.

Tips

Cleomes can be planted in groups at the back or a border or in the center of an island bed. These striking plants also make an attractive addition to a large mixed container planting.

Recommended

C. hassleriana is a tall, upright plant with strong, supple, thorny stems. The foliage and flowers of this plant have a strong, but not unpleasant, scent. Flowers are borne in loose, rounded clusters at the ends of leafy stems. Many cultivars are available.

C. serrulata (Rocky Mountain bee plant) is native to western North America but is rarely available commercially. The thorn-less dwarf cultivar **'Solo'** is regularly available to be grown from seed and grows 12–18" tall, bearing pink or white flowers.

C. hassleriana (above & below)

Cleome attracts hummingbirds and provides them with nectar well into fall because its flowers keep on blooming after many other plants have finished for the year.

Also called: spider flower
Features: attractive, scented foliage; purple, pink or white flowers; thorny stems
Height: 1–5' **Spread:** 12–24"

Cosmos

Cosmos

C. bipinnatus (above), C. sulphureus (below)

The goldfinch, the state bird of New Jersey, loves cosmos seeds and will flock to the plants as the seeds mature. Cosmos make lovely and long-lasting additions to bouquets.

With their array of bright shades, cosmos flowers add a splash of color to any garden and attract birds and butterflies.

Growing

Cosmos prefer **full sun** in a sheltered location out of the wind. The soil should be of **poor to average fertility** and **well drained**. These plants are drought tolerant, so too much water or fertilizer can reduce flowering. Sow seed directly into the garden in spring. Deadhead to encourage more flowering. Poke twiggy sticks into the ground around young seedlings to support the plants as they grow.

Tips

Cosmos make an attractive addition to cottage gardens and the back of a border. Try mass planting them in informal beds and borders.

Recommended

C. bipinnatus is a tall plant with feathery foliage. It bears flowers in many shades of pink as well as red, purple or white. Older cultivars grow 3–6' tall, while some of the newer varieties grow 12–36" tall. Many cultivars are available.

C. sulphureus (yellow cosmos) is an upright plant that bears flowers in shades of yellow, orange or red. Older cultivars grow up to 7' tall, while newer ones grow 1–4' tall. Many cultivars are available.

Features: pink, purple, red, white, yellow, orange or maroon flowers; feathery foliage
Height: 1–7' **Spread:** 12–18"

Gazania
Gazania

G. rigens hybrids (above & below)

$\mathcal{F}$ew other flowers can rival gazania for adding vivid oranges, reds and yellows to the garden and for lasting into winter.

Growing

Gazania grows best in **full sun** but tolerates some shade. The soil should be of **poor to average fertility, sandy** and **well drained**. Gazania is drought tolerant and grows best when temperatures are over 78° F. It becomes very frost tolerant by fall and often blooms into late fall and sometimes winter. Flowers may stay open only on sunny days.

Tips

Low-growing gazania makes an excellent groundcover and is also useful on exposed slopes, in mixed containers and as an edging plant in flowerbeds. It is a wonderful plant for a xeriscape or dry garden design. It is also great for patio pots, especially for gardeners who do not water as often as they should. Combine it with portulaca for a pretty effect.

Recommended

G. rigens forms a low basal rosette of lobed foliage. Large, daisy-like flowers with pointed petals are borne on strong stems above the plant. Many cultivars are available.

Features: red, orange, yellow, pink or cream flowers **Height:** usually 6–8"; may reach 12–18" **Spread:** 8–12"

Geranium
Pelargonium

P. zonale cultivar (above), P. peltatum (below)

Ivy-leaved geranium is one of the most beautiful plants to include in a mixed hanging basket. Scented geraniums on a windowsill will yield leaves for cakes and to dry for fragrance.

Tough, predictable, sun-loving and drought-resistant, geraniums have earned their place as flowering favorites in the annual garden. If you are looking for something out of the ordinary, seek out the scented geraniums with their fragrant, often decorative foliage.

Growing

Geraniums prefer **full sun** but will tolerate partial shade, though they may not bloom as profusely. The soil should be **fertile** and **well drained**. Deadheading is essential to keep geraniums blooming and looking neat.

Tips

Geraniums are very popular in borders, beds, planters, hanging baskets and window boxes. Geraniums are perennials that are treated as annuals and can be kept indoors over winter in a bright room.

Recommended

P. peltatum (ivy-leaved geranium) has thick, waxy leaves and a trailing habit. Many cultivars are available.

P. species and **cultivars** (scented geraniums, scented pelargoniums) are a large group of geraniums that have fragrant leaves. The scents are grouped into categories including rose, mint, citrus, fruit, spice and pungent.

P. zonale (zonal geranium) is a bushy plant with red, pink, purple, orange or white flowers and, frequently, banded or multi-colored foliage. Many cultivars are available.

Features: red, pink, violet, orange, salmon, white or purple flowers; decorative, sometimes scented foliage; variable habits **Height:** 8–24" **Spread:** 6"–4'

Impatiens

Impatiens

I. walleriana (above), *I. hawkeri* (below)

Impatiens are the high-wattage dar-lings of the shade garden, delivering masses of flowers in a wide variety of colors.

Growing

Impatiens do best in **partial shade** or **light shade** but tolerate full shade or, if kept moist, full sun. New Guinea impa-tiens are the best adapted to sunny loca-tions. The soil should be **fertile, humus rich, moist** and **well drained**.

Tips

Impatiens are known to flower profusely even in deep shade, so mass plant them in beds under trees, along shady fences or walls or in porch planters. They also look lovely in hanging baskets. New Guinea impatiens are grown as much for their variegated leaves as for their flowers.

Recommended

I. hawkeri (New Guinea hybrids; New Guinea impatiens) flowers in shades of red, orange, pink, purple or white. The foliage is often variegated with a yellow stripe down the center of each leaf.

I. walleriana (impatiens, busy Lizzie) flowers in shades of purple, red, bur-gundy, pink, yellow, salmon, orange, apricot, white or bicolors. Dozens of cultivars are available.

The English named I. walleriana *busy Lizzie because it flowers continuously through the growing season. It also makes a colorful windowsill plant in winter.*

Also called: busy Lizzie **Features:** flowers in shades of purple, red, burgundy, pink, yellow, salmon, orange, apricot, white or bicolors; grows well in shade **Height:** 6–36" **Spread:** 12–24"

Love-in-a-Mist

Nigella

N. damascena (above & below)

Love-in-a-mist's ferny foliage and delicate, blue flowers blend with most plants. It has a wonderful tendency to self-sow and may show up in unexpected spots in your garden for years to come.

Growing

Love-in-a-mist prefers **full sun**. The soil should be of **average fertility, light** and **well drained**. Sow seeds directly in the garden at two-week intervals all spring to prolong the blooming period.

The aromatic seeds have been used as a cooking spice and as medicine. The pods are valuable for dried floral arrangements and wreaths.

Tips

This attractive, airy plant is often used in mixed beds and borders. The flowers appear to float above the delicate foliage. Trim back the pods to keep plants blooming. The blooming may slow and the plants may die back if the weather gets too hot in summer.

The stems of this plant can be a bit floppy and may benefit from being staked with twiggy branches. Poke the branches into the dirt around the plant when it is young, and the plant will grow up between them.

Recommended

N. damascena forms a loose mound of finely divided foliage. Cultivars are available with a wider variety of flower colors than the blue offered by the species.

Also called: devil-in-a-bush
Features: feathery foliage; blue, white, pink or purple, exotic flowers **Height:** 16–24"
Spread: 8–12"

Marigold
Tagetes

From the large, exotic, ruffled flowers of African marigold to the tiny flowers on the low-growing signet marigold, the warm colors and fresh scent of marigolds add a festive touch to the garden.

Growing
Marigolds grow best in **full sun**. The soil should be of **average fertility** and **well drained**. These plants are drought tolerant but will hold up well in windy, rainy weather. Too much water will brown the blooms. Deadhead to prolong blooming and to keep plants tidy. Sow seed directly in the garden after the chance of frost has passed.

Tips
Mass planted or mixed with other plants, marigolds make a vibrant addition to beds, borders and container gardens. These plants will thrive in the hottest, driest parts of your garden and continue well into fall.

Recommended
There are many cultivars available for all the species. **T. erecta** (African marigold, American marigold, Aztec marigold) is the largest species with the biggest flowers; **T. patula** (French marigold) is low growing and has a wide range of flower colors; **T. tenuifolia** (signet marigold) has become more popular recently because of its feathery foliage and small, dainty flowers; **T. Triploid hybrids** (triploid marigold) have been developed by crossing French and African marigolds, which results in plants with huge flowers and compact growth.

T. patula 'Boy Series' (above), *T. patula* hybrid (below)

Marigolds are often included in vegetable gardens for their reputed insect- and nematode-repelling qualities. Many of them make bright cake decorations, as they are edible.

Features: bright yellow, red, orange, brown, gold, cream or bicolored flowers; fragrant foliage **Height:** 6–36" **Spread:** 12–24"

Million Bells

Calibrachoa

C. 'Trailing Blue' (above)
C. 'Trailing Pink' and 'Trailing Blue' (below)

Million bells are very charming and, given the right conditions, bloom continually during the growing season.

Growing

Million bells prefer **full sun**. The soil should be **fertile, moist** and **well drained**. Although they prefer to be watered regularly, million bells are fairly drought resistant once established. They bloom well into fall, becoming fairly cold tolerant as they mature over summer.

Tips

Popular for planters and hanging baskets, million bells are also attractive in beds and borders. They grow all summer and need plenty of room to spread, or they will overtake other flowers. Pinch back to keep plants compact.

Recommended

C. **hybrids** have a dense, trailing habit. They bear small flowers that resemble petunias, and cultivars are available with a wide range of flower colors.

The flowers close at night and on cloudy days.

Also called: calibrachoa, trailing petunia
Features: pink, purple, yellow, red-orange, white or blue flowers; trailing habit
Height: 6–12" **Spread:** up to 24"

Nasturtium
Tropaeolum

*T*hese fast-growing, brightly colored, edible flowers are easy to grow, making them popular with beginners and experienced gardeners alike.

Growing
Nasturtiums prefer **full sun** but tolerate some shade. The soil should be of **poor to average fertility, light, moist** and **well drained**. Soil that is too rich or has too much nitrogen fertilizer will result in lots of leaves but very few flowers. Water well, but let the soil drain completely between watering. Sow seeds directly in the garden once the danger of frost has passed.

Tips
Nasturtiums are used in beds, borders, containers and hanging baskets and on sloped banks. The climbing varieties are grown up trellises or over rock walls or places that need concealing. These plants thrive in poor locations, and they make an interesting addition to plantings on hard-to-mow slopes.

Recommended
T. majus has a trailing habit, but many of the cultivars have bushier, more refined habits. Cultivars offer differing flower colors or variegated foliage.

Features: bright red, orange, yellow, burgundy, pink, cream, gold, white or bicolored flowers; attractive foliage; edible leaves and flowers; varied habits **Height:** 12–18" for dwarf varieties; up to 10' for climbing varieties **Spread:** equal to height

T. majus (above), *T. majus* 'Alaska' (below)

The leaves and flowers are edible, adding a peppery flavor to salads.

Nicotiana
Nicotiana

N. x *sanderae* cultivar (above & below)

The seeds require light and warmth to germinate, so if you start plants from seed, press them into the soil surface but don't cover them.

Nicotianas were originally cultivated for the wonderful fragrance of the flowers, a feature that, in some cases, has been lost in favor of an expanded selection of flower colors. Fragrant varieties are still available.

Growing

Nicotianas grow equally well in **full sun, light shade** or **partial shade**. The soil should be **fertile, rich in organic matter, moist** and **well drained**.

Tips

Nicotianas are popular in beds and borders. The dwarf varieties do well in containers. Do not plant nicotianas near tomatoes because, as members of the same plant family, they share a vulnerability to many of the same diseases. Nicotiana plants may attract and harbor diseases that will hardly affect them but that can kill tomatoes.

Recommended

N. x *sanderae* (*N. alata* x *N. forgetiana*) is a hybrid from which many brightly colored and dwarf cultivars have been developed.

N. sylvestris grows up to 4' tall and bears white blooms that are fragrant in the evening.

Also called: flowering tobacco plant
Features: red, pink, green, yellow, white or purple, sometimes fragrant flowers
Height: 1–5' **Spread:** 12"

Pansy
Viola

V. x wittrockiana (above & below)

Colorful and cheerful, pansy flowers are a welcome sight in spring after a long, dreary winter.

Growing

Pansies prefer **full sun** but tolerate partial shade. The soil should be **fertile, moist** and **well drained**. Pansies do best when the weather is cool and may die back over summer. They may rejuvenate in late summer, but it is often easier to pull up faded plants and replace them with new ones in fall. These may very well survive winter and provide you with flowers again in spring.

Tips

Pansies can be used in beds and borders, and they are popular for mixing in with spring-flowering bulbs and primroses. They can also be grown in containers.

Recommended

V. x wittrockiana is a small, bushy plant that bears flowers in a wide range of bright and pastel colors, often with markings on the petals that give the flowers a face-like appearance.

Pansy petals are edible and make delightful garnishes for salads and desserts.

Features: flowers in bright or pastel shades of blue, purple, red, orange, yellow, pink, white or bicolors **Height:** 6–12" **Spread:** 6–12"

Petunia

Petunia

P. 'Lavender Wave' (above), *P.* multiflora type (below)

For speedy growth, prolific bloom-ing and ease of care, petunias are hard to beat.

Growing

Petunias prefer **full sun**. The soil should be of **average to rich fertility, light, sandy** and **well drained**. Pinch halfway back in mid-summer to keep plants bushy and to encourage new growth and flowers.

Tips

Use petunias in beds, borders, contain-ers and hanging baskets.

Recommended

P. x *hybrida* is a large group of popular, sun-loving annuals that fall into three categories: **grandifloras** have the largest flowers in the widest range of colors, but they can be damaged by rain; **multifloras** bear more flowers that are smaller and less easily damaged by heavy rain; and **millifloras** have the smallest flowers in the narrowest range of colors, but they are the most prolific and least likely to be damaged by heavy rain.

Features: pink, purple, red, white, yellow, coral, blue or bicolored flowers; versatile
Height: 6–18" **Spread:** 12–24" or wider

Poppy
Papaver

*P*oppies seem to have been made to grow in groups. The many flowers swaying in the breeze seem to be having lively conversations with one another.

Growing

Poppies grow best in **full sun**. The soil should be **average to fertile, humus rich** and **well drained**. Sow seeds directly in the garden every two weeks in spring. The tiny seeds can be mixed with fine sand to make it easier to spread them out evenly. Poppies will self-sow if allowed to go to seed, so you may have to plant them only once.

Tips

Poppies work well in mixed borders where other plants are slow to fill in. The poppies fill the empty spaces in early summer and then die back as summer heats up, leaving room for other plants. They are also ideal for naturalizing in a meadow or rock garden where they will re-seed year after year.

Recommended

P. rhoeas (field poppy, corn poppy, Memorial Day poppy, Flanders poppy) forms a basal rosette of foliage above which flowers in a wide range of colors are borne on long stems. This species is the bright red poppy that blooms for Memorial Day.

P. somniferum (opium poppy) bears red, pink, white or purple, single or double flowers. The black or blue seeds of this "bread poppy" are used for baking. Although propagation of the species is restricted in many countries because

P. somniferum 'Peony Flowered' (above)
P. rhoeas (below)

of its narcotic properties, several attractive cultivars have been developed for ornamental and culinary use.

California poppy (Eschscholtzia californica) is a related annual that forms a mound of delicate, feathery, blue-green foliage. It bears satiny, orange or yellow flowers all summer. It grows in poor soils and freely self-seeds.

Features: orange, yellow, red, pink, purple or white flowers; attractive foliage
Height: 12–24" **Spread:** 12–18"

Portulaca

Portulaca

For a brilliant show in the hottest, driest, poorest, most neglected area of your garden, you can't go wrong with portulaca.

Growing

Portulaca requires **full sun**. The soil should be of **poor fertility, sandy** and **well drained**. To ensure that you will have plants where you want them, start seed indoors or buy a flat at your local garden center. If you sow the tiny seeds directly outdoors, rain may wash them away, and the plants will pop up in unexpected places.

Tips

Portulaca is the ideal plant for garden spots that just don't get enough water—under the eaves of the house or in dry, rocky, exposed areas. Do not mulch, and it will re-seed. It is also ideal for people who like baskets hanging from the front porch, but who forget to water regularly. They will still need to be watered occasionally, but as long as the location is sunny, this plant will do well with minimal care.

Recommended

P. grandiflora forms a bushy mound of succulent foliage. It bears delicate, papery, rose-like flowers profusely all summer. Many cultivars are available, including some that have flowers that stay open on cloudy days.

P. grandiflora (above & below)

Spacing the plants closely together is not a problem; in fact, the intertwining of the plants creates an interesting and attractive effect.

Also called: moss rose **Features:** drought-resistant, summer flowers in shades of red, pink, yellow, white, purple, orange or peach **Height:** 4–8" **Spread:** 6–12" or wider

Salvia

Salvia

Salvias should be part of every annual garden. The attractive and varied forms have something to offer every style of yard.

Growing

All salvia plants prefer **full sun** but will tolerate light shade. The soil should be **average to fertile, humus rich, moist** and **well drained**. To keep plants producing flowers, deadhead, water often and fertilize monthly.

Tips

Salvias look good grouped in beds and borders and in containers. The flowers are long lasting and make good cut flowers for fresh arrangements. Some also dry well.

Recommended

S. argentea (silver sage) is grown for its large, fuzzy, silvery leaves. *S. coccinea* (Texas sage) is a bushy, upright plant that bears whorled spikes of white, pink, blue or purple flowers. *S. farinacea* (mealy cup sage, blue sage) has bright blue flowers clustered along stems powdered with silver. Cultivars are available. *S. splendens* (salvia, scarlet sage) is grown for its spikes of bright red, tubular flowers. Recently, cultivars have become available in white, pink, purple or orange. *S. viridis* (*S. horminium*; annual clary sage) is grown for its pink, purple, blue or white bracts, rather than the tiny flowers within the bracts.

S. splendens (above), S. farinacea 'Victoria' (below)

There are over 900 species of Salvia.

Also called: sage **Features:** red, blue, purple, burgundy, pink, orange, salmon, yellow, cream, white or bicolored, summer flowers; attractive foliage **Height:** 8"–4'
Spread: 8"–4'

Snapdragon
Antirrhinum

A. majus cultivar (above & below)

Snapdragons are perennials that are treated like annuals. Although they usually won't survive most winters here, they will often flower well into fall and may self-seed.

Snapdragons are among the most appealing plants. The flower colors are always rich and vibrant, and even the most jaded gardeners are tempted to squeeze open the dragons' mouths.

Growing
Snapdragons prefer **full sun** but tolerate light shade or partial shade. The soil should be **fertile, rich in organic matter, neutral to alkaline** and **well drained**. Do not cover seeds when sowing because they require light for germination. For a quick start, purchase flats of plants in May.

To encourage bushy growth, pinch the tips of young plants. Cut off the flower spikes as they fade to promote further blooming and to prevent the plant from dying back before the end of the season.

Tips
The height of the variety dictates the best place for it in a border—the shortest varieties work well near the front, and the tallest look good in the centre or back. The dwarf and medium-height varieties can also be used in planters. A trailing variety does well in hanging baskets.

Recommended
There are many cultivars of **A. majus** available, generally grouped into three size categories: dwarf, medium and giant. They all bear spikes of colorful flowers.

Features: white, cream, yellow, orange, red, maroon, pink, purple or bicolored, entertaining flowers **Height:** 6"–4' **Spread:** 6–24"

Sunflower

Helianthus

There are so many sunflower options, and I have never seen one I didn't like. The more the merrier.

Growing

Sunflowers grow best in **full sun**. The soil should be of **average fertility, humus rich, moist** and **well drained**.

Sunflowers are excellent for children to grow. The seeds are big and easy to handle, and they germinate quickly. The plants grow continually upward, and their progress can be measured until the flower finally appears at the top of the tall plant. If planted along the wall of a two-story house, beneath an upstairs window, the progress can be observed from above as well as below, and the flowers will be easier to see.

Tips

The low-growing varieties can be used in beds and borders. The tall varieties are effective at the backs of borders and make good screens and temporary hedges. The tallest varieties may need staking.

Recommended

H. annuus (common sunflower) is considered weedy, but many attractive cultivars have been developed.

Birds will flock to the ripening seed heads of your sunflowers, quickly plucking out the tightly packed seeds.

H. annuus 'Teddy Bear' (above)
H. annuus cultivar (below)

Features: late-summer flowers, most commonly yellow, but also orange, red, brown, cream or bicolored, typically with brown, purple or rusty red centers; edible seeds
Height: 24" for dwarf varieties; up to 15' for giant varieties **Spread:** 12–24"

Sweet Alyssum
Lobularia

L. maritima cultivars (above & below)

Sweet alyssum is excellent for creating soft edges, and it self-seeds, popping up along pathways and between stones late in the season to give summer a sweet sendoff.

Growing

Sweet alyssum prefers **full sun** but tolerates light shade. **Well-drained** soil of **average fertility** is preferred, but poor soil is tolerated. Sweet alyssum may die back a bit during the heat and humidity of summer. Trim it back, provide a light mulch and water it periodically to encourage new growth and more flowers when the weather cools.

Tips

Sweet alyssum creeps around rock gardens, over stone walls and along the edges of beds. It is an excellent choice for seeding into cracks and crevices of walkways and between patio stones, and once established it readily re-seeds. It is also good for filling in spaces between taller plants in borders and mixed containers.

Recommended

L. maritima forms a low, spreading mound of foliage. The entire plant appears to be covered in tiny blossoms when in full flower. Cultivars with flowers in a wide range of colors are available.

Leave alyssum plants out all winter. In spring, remove the previous year's growth to expose self-sown seedlings below.

Features: pink, purple, yellow, salmon, apricot or white, fragrant flowers **Height:** 3–12" **Spread:** 6–24"

Verbena

Verbena

Verbenas offer butterflies a banquet. Butterfly visitors include tiger swallowtails, silver-spotted skippers, great spangled fritillaries and painted ladies.

Growing

Verbenas grow best in **full sun**. The soil should be **fertile** and very **well drained**. Pinch back young plants for bushy growth.

Tips

Use verbenas on rock walls and in beds, borders, rock gardens, containers, hanging baskets and window boxes. They make good substitutes for ivy-leaved geraniums where the sun is hot and where a roof overhang keeps the mildew-prone verbenas dry. They do best where constant lawn irrigation doesn't hit them.

Recommended

V. bonariensis forms a low clump of foliage from which tall, stiff stems bear clusters of small, purple flowers.

V. x *hybrida* is a bushy plant that may be upright or spreading. It bears clusters of small flowers in a wide range of colors. Cultivars are available.

If plants become leggy or overgrown, cut them back by half to tidy them up and to promote the production of lots of fall blooms.

V. bonariensis (above), *V.* x *hybrida* (below)

Also called: garden verbena **Features:** red, pink, purple, blue, yellow, scarlet, silver, peach or white flowers, some with white centers **Height:** 8"–5' **Spread:** 12–36"

Vinca

Catharanthus

C. roseus (above & below)

Vinca is tolerant of dry spells, searing sun and city pollution. It exhibits grace under all sorts of pressure.

Growing

Vinca prefers **full sun** but tolerates partial shade. Any **well-drained** soil is fine. This plant endures pollution and drought but prefers to be watered regularly. It doesn't like to be too wet or too cold. Avoid planting vinca until the soil has warmed because it may fail to thrive if planted in cold or wet soil.

Tips

Vinca will do well in the sunniest, warmest part of the garden. Plant it in a bed along an exposed driveway or against the south-facing wall of a house. It can also be used in hanging baskets, in planters and as a temporary groundcover.

Recommended

C. roseus (*Vinca rosea*) forms a mound of strong stems. The flowers are pink, red or white, often with contrasting centers. Many cultivars are available.

One of the best annuals to use in front of homes on busy streets, Vinca rosea *will bloom happily despite exposure to exhaust fumes and dust. It should not be confused with the groundcover* Vinca minor.

Also called: Madagascar periwinkle
Features: attractive foliage; flowers in shades of red, rose, pink, mauve or white, often with contrasting centers; durable
Height: 6–24" **Spread:** usually equal to or greater than height

Zinnia

Zinnia

*Z*innia blooms are such wonderful wheels of color that they should be included in every sunny garden.

Growing

Zinnias grow best in **full sun**. The soil should be **fertile, humus rich, moist** and **well drained**. They are one of the easiest annuals to start from seed and can be transplanted easily if the soil is moistened. You can sow seeds directly in the garden when soil warms or start them indoors in individual peat pots for an early batch of plants. Plant another row directly in the garden when soil is warmest for a later crop of flowers. Try to avoid constant lawn irrigation to steer clear of mildew on foliage. Deadhead to prolong blooming and to keep plants looking neat.

Tips

Zinnias are useful in beds, borders, containers and cutting gardens. The dwarf selections can be used as edging plants. Zinnias provide wonderful fall color.

Recommended

Z. elegans is a bushy, upright plant with daisy-like flowers in a variety of forms and colors. Heights vary from 6–36". Many cultivars are available, though mildew-resistant cultivars are the best choice.

Z. haageana (Mexican zinnia) is a bushy plant with narrow leaves that bears bicolored or tricolored, daisy-like flowers in shades of orange, red, yellow, maroon, brown or gold. Plants grow 12–24" tall. Cultivars are available.

Z. elegans cultivars (above & below)

Mildew can be a problem for zinnias, so choose mildew-resistant cultivars and grow them in locations with good air circulation.

Features: bushy habit; flowers in shades of red, yellow, green, purple, orange, pink, white, maroon, brown or gold, sometimes bicolored or tricolored **Height:** 6–36" **Spread:** 12–18"

Aster

Aster

A. novae-angliae (above), A. novi-belgii (below)

Among the final plants to bloom before the snow flies, asters often provide a last meal for migrating butterflies. The purples, blues and pinks of asters make a nice contrast to the yellow-flowered perennials common in the late-summer garden.

Growing

Asters prefer **full sun** but tolerate partial shade. The soil should be **fertile, moist** and **well drained**. Trim plants back by 6–8" at least once in early summer to promote bushy growth and to extend the fall bloom. Pinching must be done before mid-July, or blooming will be reduced. Mulch in winter to protect plants from temperature fluctuations. Divide every two to three years to maintain vigor and to control spread.

Tips

Use asters in the middle of borders and in cottage gardens, or naturalize them in wild gardens.

Recommended

Some *Aster* species have been reclassified under the genus *Symphyotrichum*. You may see both names at garden centers.

A. novae-angliae (Michaelmas daisy, New England aster) is an upright, spreading, clump-forming perennial that bears yellow-centered, purple flowers. Many cultivars are available.

A. novi-belgii (Michaelmas daisy, New York aster) is a dense, upright, clump-forming perennial with purple flowers. Many cultivars are available.

A. oblongifolius (aromatic aster) is a bushy, mound-forming perennial with fragrant foliage. It bears flowers in shades of blue and purple in late summer and fall. Cultivars are available.

Features: late-summer to mid-fall flowers in shades of red, white, blue, purple or pink, often with yellow centers **Height:** 10"–5' **Spread:** 18–36" **Hardiness:** zones 3–8

Astilbe

Astilbe

Astilbes, especially those with white blooms that glisten and sparkle, are beacons in the shade. Their high-impact flowers will brighten any gloomy section of your garden.

Growing

Astilbes grow best in **light shade** or **partial shade** but tolerate full shade, though they will not flower as much. The soil should be **fertile, humus rich, acidic, moist** and **well drained**. Add compost to increase the organic matter in the soil. Although astilbes appreciate moist soil, they don't like standing water. They are heavy feeders and may need a couple of applications of 5–10–5 fertilizer during spring and summer.

Astilbes should be divided every three years or so to maintain plant vigor. Root masses may lift out of the soil as they mature. Add a layer of topsoil and mulch if this occurs.

Tips

Astilbes can be grown near the edges of bog gardens and ponds and in woodland gardens and shaded borders.

Recommended

A. x *arendsii* (astilbe, false spirea, Arend's astilbe) is a group of many variable hybrids with foliage in shades from light green to bronze and flowers in a wide range of shades including white, cream, red, pink and purple.

A. x *arendsii* cultivars (above)
A. x *arendsii* 'Bressingham Beauty' (below)

A. chinensis (Chinese astilbe) is a dense, vigorous perennial that tolerates dry soil better than other astilbe species. Its flowers are pale pink. **Var. *pumila*** is a dwarf selection with reddish green leaves and reddish pink flowers.

A. simplicifolia 'Sprite' is a clump-forming perennial with finely divided, feathery foliage. Delicate, airy, slightly pendulous, light pink flower clusters are borne in summer.

Features: attractive foliage; white, pink, purple, peach or red, summer flowers
Height: 10"–4' **Spread:** 8–36"
Hardiness: zones 3–9

Bellflower

Campanula

C. persicifolia (above)
C. carpatica 'White Clips' (below)

T hanks to their wide range of heights and habits, it is possible to put bellflowers almost anywhere in the garden. For those seeking blue flowers, there are many shades of blue among bellflowers.

Growing

Bellflowers grow well in **full sun, partial shade** or **light shade**. The soil should be of **average to rich fertility** and **well drained**. These plants appreciate mulch to keep their roots cool and moist in summer and protected in winter, particularly if snow cover is inconsistent. Deadhead to prolong blooming.

Tips

Plant upright and mounding bellflowers in borders and cottage gardens. Use low, spreading and trailing bellflowers in rock gardens and on rock walls. You can also edge beds with the low-growing varieties.

Recommended

C. x **'Birch Hybrid'** is a low-growing, spreading plant. It bears light blue to mauve flowers in summer.

C. carpatica (Carpathian bellflower, Carpathian harebell) is a spreading, mounding perennial that bears blue, white or purple flowers in summer. Several cultivars are available.

C. glomerata (clustered bellflower) forms a clump of upright stems and bears clusters of purple, blue or white flowers throughout most of summer.

C. persicifolia (peach-leaved bellflower) is an upright perennial that bears white, blue or purple flowers from early to mid-summer.

C. poscharskyana (Serbian bellflower) is a trailing plant. It bears light violet blue flowers in summer and early fall.

Also called: campanula **Features:** blue, white, purple or pink, spring, summer or fall flowers; varied growing habits **Height:** 4"–6' **Spread:** 12–36" **Hardiness:** zones 3–7

Black-Eyed Susan

Rudbeckia

Black-eyed Susan is a tough, low-maintenance, long-lived perennial loved by butterflies and goldfinches. It will surprise you with its stellar performance even in shady spots.

Growing

Black-eyed Susan grows well in **full sun** or **partial shade**. The soil should be of **average fertility** and **well drained**. Some *Rudbeckia* species are touted as "claybusters" for their tolerance of fairly heavy clay soils. Established plants are drought tolerant but prefer to have a regular source of water. Divide them in fall every three to five years.

Tips

Include these native plants in wildflower and natural gardens, beds and borders. Pinching the plants in early June will encourage lower, bushier growth but can somewhat delay flowering. Try pinching only half of each plant to really extend the bloom time.

Recommended

R. fulgida is an upright, spreading plant that bears orange-yellow flowers with brown centers. **Var. *sullivantii* 'Goldsturm'** bears large, golden yellow flowers.

R. laciniata (cutleaf coneflower) forms a large, open clump of stems and deeply cut leaves. The flowers are yellow with green centers. **'Goldquelle'** has bright yellow, double flowers.

R. nitida is an upright, spreading plant with green-centered, yellow flowers.

R. fulgida (above), *R. nitida* 'Herbstsonne' (below)

Cultivars of R. hirta are often grown as annuals, offering plentiful blooms in a wider range of colors.

Features: yellow or orange-yellow flowers with brown or green centers; attractive foliage; easy to grow **Height:** 2–6' **Spread:** 18–36" **Hardiness:** zones 3–8

Bleeding Heart
Dicentra

D. formosa (above), D. spectabilis (below)

Every garden should have a spot for a bleeding heart. Tucked away in a shady spot, this lovely plant appears in spring and fills the garden with fresh promise.

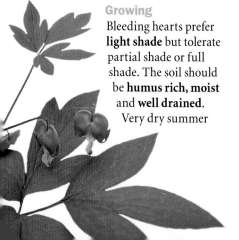

Growing

Bleeding hearts prefer **light shade** but tolerate partial shade or full shade. The soil should be **humus rich, moist** and **well drained**. Very dry summer conditions cause the plants to die back, though some varieties revive in fall and others the following spring. Bleeding hearts must remain moist while blooming in order to prolong the flowering period. Regular watering will keep the flowers coming until mid-summer.

Tips

Bleeding hearts can be naturalized in a woodland garden or grown in a border or rock garden. They make excellent early-season specimen plants and do well near ponds or streams. These plants thrive near a birdbath, where they can be assured of getting a "drink" each day.

Recommended

D. eximia (fringed bleeding heart) forms a loose, mounded clump of lacy, fern-like foliage and bears pink or white flowers in spring and sporadically over summer.

D. formosa (western bleeding heart) is a low-growing, wide-spreading plant with pink or rose red flowers. The most drought tolerant of the bleeding hearts, it is the most likely to continue flowering all summer.

D. 'Luxuriant' is a low-growing hybrid with blue-green foliage and red-pink blooms that last from spring to summer.

D. spectabilis (common bleeding heart, Japanese bleeding heart) forms a large, elegant mound that bears flowers with white inner petals and pink outer petals. Several cultivars are available. This one goes dormant over summer.

Features: pink, white, red or purple, spring and summer flowers; attractive foliage
Height: 1–4' **Spread:** 12–36"
Hardiness: zones 3–9

Butterfly Weed

Asclepias

These brilliantly colored North American natives are a major food source for monarch butterflies, both larvae and adults.

Growing

Butterfly weeds grow best in **full sun**. The soil should be very **well drained**. Some selections like more moisture. *A. tuberosa* is very drought tolerant. Deadhead to encourage a second flush of blooms, but leave the second flush of flowers to go to seed. Plants resent being divided, but seedlings can be transplanted as needed to propagate them.

Tips

Use *A. tuberosa* in meadow plantings and borders, on dry banks, in neglected areas and in wildflower, cottage and butterfly gardens. Use *A. incarnata* in moist borders and in bog, pond-side or stream-side plantings.

Recommended

A. incarnata (swamp milkweed) forms a dense clump of thick stems. It bears clusters of pink, white or light purple flowers in late spring or early summer. Cultivars are available.

A. tuberosa (butterfly weed) forms a clump of upright, leafy stems. It bears clusters of orange flowers from mid-summer to early fall. Cultivars are available. This roadside beauty thrives in the typical south Jersey sand with little or no extra care.

A. incarnata (above), *A. tuberosa* (below)

There are also tender and annual species of Asclepias *available.* A. curassavica *(blood flower) and* A. physocarpa *(swan plant) are two that are popular and commonly available and also loved by butterflies.*

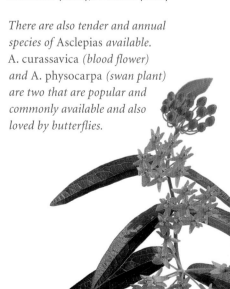

Also called: milkweed, pleurisy root, railroad Annie **Features:** red, yellow, orange, white, pink or light purple flowers; attracts butterflies **Height:** 18–36" **Spread:** 12–24" **Hardiness:** zones 4–9

Cardinal Flower
Lobelia

L. cardinalis (above & below)

These beauties are a must for late-summer color. The brilliant red of their flowers is motivation enough for some gardeners to install a pond or bog garden just to better meet cardinal flower's moist soil requirements.

These lovely members of the bellflower family contain deadly alkaloids and have poisoned people who tried to use them in herbal medicines.

Growing

Cardinal flowers grow well in **full sun, light shade** or **partial shade**. The soil should be **fertile, slightly acidic** and **moist**. Avoid letting the soil dry out completely, especially in a sunny location. Mulch plants lightly in winter for protection. Deadhead to keep the plants neat and to encourage a possible second flush of blooms. Plants tend to self-seed, which is a real plus with this wonderful plant. Seedlings can be moved to new locations or left where they are to replace the short-lived parent plants when they die.

Tips

These plants are best suited to stream-side or pondside plantings or in bog gardens. They can also be included in moist beds and borders or in any location where they will be watered regularly. However, sometimes they surprise you by seeding themselves in a drier area and growing wherever they come up, perhaps "forgetting" that they love moisture.

Recommended

L. cardinalis forms an upright clump of bronzy green leaves and bears spikes of bright red flowers from summer to fall. There are also many hybrids and cultivars available, often with flowers in shades of blue, purple, deep burgundy red or pink.

Features: bright red, purple, blue or pink, summer flowers; bronzy green foliage
Height: 2–4' **Spread:** 12–24"
Hardiness: zones 4–9

Christmas Rose

Helleborus

This wonderful plant is as tough as nails and will provide interest all year long. It blooms from December until spring, hence its common names, Christmas and Lenten rose.

Growing

Christmas roses prefer **light shade** and a sheltered location but tolerate some direct sun if the soil stays evenly moist. The soil should be **fertile, humus rich, moist** and **well drained**. Although they are said to prefer neutral to alkaline soil, they seem to thrive in the acidic soil of a New Jersey woodland site. A soggy, wet site is about the only place they will not thrive. Mulch plants in winter if they are in an exposed location. Cut off the previous year's foliage when the new flower buds appear.

Tips

Use these plants in a sheltered border or rock garden, or naturalize them in a woodland garden. Christmas roses are deer-resistant.

Recommended

H. foetidus is an upright plant with very attractive, finely dissected foliage that smells unpleasant when crushed. It bears clusters of green, sometimes fragrant flowers from mid-winter to spring. It grows up to 32" tall. (Zones 6–9)

H. x *hybridus* plants grow about 18" tall, may be deciduous or evergreen and bloom in a wide range of colors. Cultivars can have single or double, spotted, picotee or ruffled flowers in light or deep shades. (Zones 5–9)

H. orientalis cultivar (above), *H. foetidus* (below)

H. niger (Christmas rose) and *H. orientalis* (Lenten rose) form clumps of evergreen foliage. Christmas rose grows about 12" tall and bears upward-facing flowers in late winter or early spring. Lenten rose grows 12–24" tall and bears flowers in mid- to late spring. The flowers of both are white or greenish white and turn pink as they age.

Features: white, green, pink, purple or yellow, winter to spring flowers; evergreen foliage
Height: 12–32" **Spread:** 18"
Hardiness: zones 4–9

Columbine

Aquilegia

*elicate and beautiful, columbines will naturalize and add a touch of simple elegance to any garden. Blooming from the cool of spring through to mid-summer, these long-lasting flowers herald the passing of spring and the arrival of warm summer weather.

Growing

Columbines grow well in **light shade** or **partial shade**. They prefer soil that is **fertile, moist** and **well drained**, but they adapt to most soil conditions. Division is not required but can be done to propagate desirable plants. The divided plants may take a while to recover because columbines dislike having their roots disturbed.

Tips

Use columbines in rock gardens, formal or casual borders and naturalized or woodland gardens.

Recommended

A. canadensis (wild columbine, Canada columbine) is a native plant that is common in woodlands and fields. It bears yellow flowers with red spurs.

A. x hybrida (*A. x cultorum*; hybrid columbine) forms mounds of delicate foliage and has exceptional flowers. Many hybrids have been developed with showy flowers in a wide range of colors.

A. vulgaris (European columbine, common columbine) has been used to develop many hybrids and cultivars with flowers in a variety of colors.

A. canadensis (above)
A. x hybrida 'McKana Giants' (below)

Columbines self-seed but are not invasive. Each year, a few new seedlings may turn up near the parent plant and can be transplanted.

Features: red, yellow, pink, purple, blue or white, spring and summer flowers; color of spurs often differs from that of petals; attractive foliage **Height:** 18–36" **Spread:** 12–24" **Hardiness:** zones 3–9

Coneflower

Echinacea

Coneflower is a visual delight, with its mauve petals offset by a spiky, orange center. The many sunset colors now available are also very garden-worthy.

Growing

Coneflower grows well in **full sun** or very **light shade**. It tolerates any **well-drained** soil, but prefers an **average to rich** soil. The thick taproots make this plant drought resistant, but it prefers to have regular water. Divide every four years or so in spring or fall. Deadhead and pinch back plants early in the flowering season to prolong blooming.

Tips

Use coneflower in meadow gardens and informal borders. Be sure to allow for air circulation to avoid mildew.

The dry flowerheads make an interesting feature in fall and winter gardens and can also be used in wreaths and flower arrangements.

Recommended

Many species, cultivars and hybrids are available. *E.* **'Double Decker'** has deep rose-colored flowers. Out of the central cone grows a second set of petals, producing a madcap effect. *E.* **'Harvest Moon'** has golden yellow petals surrounding an orange-yellow center. *E.* ORANGE MEADOWBRIGHT (**'Art's Pride'**) bears deep orange flowers with reddish orange centers. *E. purpurea* is an upright plant with prickly hairs all over. It bears purple flowers with orange

E. purpurea 'Magnus' and 'White Swan' (above)
E. purpurea (below)

centers. Two of its popular cultivars include **'Kim's Knee High,'** a low-growing, bushy cultivar, and **'White Swan,'** a compact cultivar with white flowers. *E.* **'Sunset'** produces huge, sweetly fragrant, bright orange flowers that are very attractive to butterflies. *E.* **'Twilight'** bears dark pink flowers with striking red centers.

Also called: purple coneflower, echinacea
Features: purple, pink or white, mid-summer to fall flowers with rusty orange centers; persistent seedheads **Height:** 2–5'
Spread: 12–24" **Hardiness:** zones 3–8

Daylily
Hemerocallis

H. 'Stella de Oro' (above), H. 'Bonanza' (below)

The daylily's adaptability and dura-bility, combined with its variety in color, blooming period, size and texture, explain its popularity.

Growing

Daylilies grow in any light from **full sun to full shade**. The deeper the shade, the fewer flowers will be produced. The soil should be **fertile, moist** and **well drained**, but these plants adapt to most conditions and are hard to kill once

Daylily blooms are edible and delicious filled with a creamy cheese dip.

established. Frequent spraying from lawn irrigation may cause brown spots or rot. Divide every two to three years to keep plants vigorous and to propagate them. They can, however, be left indefi-nitely without dividing.

Tips

Plant daylilies alone or in groups to nat-uralize in woodland sites, on banks and in ditches to control erosion. Small vari-eties are nice in planters.

Recommended

Daylilies come in an almost infinite number of forms, sizes and colors in a range of species, cultivars and hybrids. Consider the reblooming selections whenever possible for the longest-lasting display. See your local garden center or daylily grower to find out what's available.

Features: spring and summer flowers in every color except blue and pure white; grass-like foliage **Height:** 1–4' **Spread:** 1–4'
Hardiness: zones 2–9

Foamflower
Tiarella

T. cordifolia (above & below)

Foamflowers are natives that form handsome groundcovers in shaded areas, with attractive leaves that color nicely in fall and prolific, delicate, star-shaped, white flowers. They are very showy and bloom for a long time.

Growing

Foamflowers prefer **full shade, light shade** or **partial shade** without after-noon sun. The soil should be **humus rich, moist** and **slightly acidic**. These plants adapt to most soils. Divide in spring. Deadhead to encourage repeat blooming. If the foliage fades or rusts in summer, cut it partway to the ground, and new growth will emerge.

Tips

Foamflowers are excellent groundcovers and will naturalize in shaded and wood-land gardens.

Recommended

T. cordifolia is a low-growing, spreading plant that bears spikes of foamy-looking, white flowers. Many new cultivars and hybrids with beautifully colored leaves are available.

T. 'Maple Leaf' is a clump-forming hybrid with bronzy green, maple-like leaves and pink-flushed flowers.

Native Americans made tea from the leaves to cure mouth sores and eye ailments and to use as an astringent. Root tea was used to treat stomach and intestinal ailments.

Features: white or pink, spring and some-times early-summer flowers; decorative foliage
Height: 4–12" **Spread:** 12–24"
Hardiness: zones 3–8

Foxglove
Digitalis

D. purpurea (above & below)

Romantic foxgloves make a perfect foil for the daisy family members so common in the summer landscape.

Growing

Foxgloves grow well in **partial shade** or **light shade**. The soil should be **fertile, acidic, humus rich** and **moist**. Purple foxglove is short-lived but self-seeding and will continue to appear year after year. Remember to wear gloves when handling these toxic plants.

Tips

Foxgloves are must-haves for the cottage garden and for people interested in heritage plants. They make excellent vertical accents along the back of a border and make interesting additions to woodland gardens.

Recommended

D. grandiflora (yellow foxglove) forms a clump of glossy foliage. The 24–36" flower spikes bear large, light yellow to butter yellow flowers in early summer.

D. x *mertonensis* (strawberry foxglove) is a true perennial that forms a clump of glossy foliage. It bears spikes of large, rusty rose, tubular blooms in late spring and early summer.

D. purpurea (purple foxglove) forms a basal rosette of foliage from which tall spikes of tubular flowers emerge. The early-summer flowers come in a wide range of colors and often bear contrasting spots on their insides. Many cultivars are available.

Features: perennial or biennial; spring to early-summer flowers in shades of purple, pink, maroon, rusty rose, yellow or white; attracts hummingbirds **Height:** 2–5' **Spread:** 12–24" **Hardiness:** zones 3–8

Fragrant Violet

Viola

V. odorata (above & below)

This lovely, diminutive plant is truly the plant of poets and romantics. Besides being food for the romantic imagination, it is used in perfume, to treat cancer and as candied decorations for cakes.

Growing

Fragrant violets grow well in **partial shade**. The soil should be **fertile, humus rich, moist** and **well drained**. Plants self-seed freely and can unfortunately hybridize with wild and scentless violets, with the loss of fragrance in the off-spring. Avoid planting them near these other violets.

Tips

Fragrant violets make a lovely addition to a woodland garden, where they can be left to naturalize. In beds and borders they add a splash of color along with your favorite early-flowering bulbs.

Recommended

V. odorata is a low, spreading, semi-evergreen perennial. The dark green leaves are heart-shaped to rounded, and the sweetly scented, late-winter and early-spring flowers are white, purple or blue. **'Queen Charlotte'** is an extremely fragrant selection with dark blue flowers. **Var. *rosea*** is a pink-flowered form.

The fragrant violet goes far back in history and might be considered timeless by some. Its scent is wonderful and has been used in the perfume industry. Many fragrant cultivars were lost once the fragrant chemical was isolated and synthesized and interest waned.

Also called: sweet violet, English violet
Features: fragrant, late-winter and early-spring flowers in shades of purple, blue or white; attractive mound of dark green foliage
Height: 8" **Spread:** 8–12"
Hardiness: zones 4–8

Hardy Geranium
Geranium

G. *sanguineum* var. *striatum* (above)
G. *sanguineum* (below)

There is a type of geranium that suits every garden, thanks to the beauty and diversity of this hardy plant.

Growing

Hardy geraniums grow well in **full sun, partial shade** or **light shade**. These plants dislike hot weather and prefer **well-drained** soil of **average fertility**. *G. renardii* prefers a poor, well-drained soil. Divide in spring.

Tips

These long-flowering plants are great in a border; they fill in the spaces between shrubs and other large plants and keep the weeds down. They can be included in rock gardens and woodland gardens or mass planted as groundcovers.

Recommended

G. 'Brookside' is a clump-forming, drought-tolerant geranium with finely cut leaves and deep blue to violet blue flowers.

G. macrorrhizum (bigroot geranium, scented cranesbill) forms a spreading mound of fragrant foliage and bears flowers in various shades of pink. Cultivars are available.

G. renardii (Renard's geranium) forms a clump of velvety, deeply veined, crinkled foliage. A few white, purple-veined flowers appear over summer, but the foliage remains the main attraction.

G. sanguineum (bloodred cranesbill, bloody cranesbill) forms a dense, mounding clump and bears bright magenta flowers. Many cultivars are available.

Also called: cranesbill geranium
Features: white, red, pink, purple or blue, summer flowers; attractive, sometimes fragrant foliage **Height:** 4–36" **Spread:** 12–36"
Hardiness: zones 3–8

Heuchera

Heuchera

From soft yellow-greens and oranges to midnight purples and silvery, dappled maroons, heucheras offer a great variety of foliage options for a perennial garden with partial shade.

Growing

Heucheras grow best in **light shade** or **partial shade**. The foliage colors can bleach out in full sun, and plants grow leggy in full shade. The soil should be of **average to rich fertility, humus rich, neutral to alkaline, moist** and **well drained**. Good air circulation is essential. Deadhead to prolong the bloom time.

Every two or three years, heucheras should be dug up and the oldest, woodiest roots and stems removed. Plants may be divided at this time, if desired, then replanted with the crown at or just above soil level.

Tips

Use heucheras as edging plants, in clusters in woodland gardens or as groundcovers in low-traffic areas. Combine different foliage types for an interesting display.

Recommended

There are dozens of beautiful cultivars available with almost limitless variations in foliage markings and colors. See your local garden center or mail-order catalog to find out what is available.

H. x brizoides 'Firefly' (above), *H. sanguineum* (below)

Heucheras have a strange habit of pushing themselves up out of the soil because of their shallow root systems. Mulch in fall if the plants begin heaving from the ground.

Also called: coral bells, alum root
Features: very decorative foliage; red, pink, white, yellow or purple, spring or summer flowers **Height:** 1–4' **Spread:** 6–18"
Hardiness: zones 3–9

Hosta

Hosta

Breeders are always looking for new variations in hosta foliage. Swirls, stripes, puckers and ribs enhance the leaves' various sizes, shapes and colors.

Growing

Hostas prefer **light shade** or **partial shade** but will grow in **full shade**. Morning sun is preferable to afternoon sun in partial shade situations. The soil should ideally be **fertile, moist** and **well drained**, but most soils are tolerated. Hostas are fairly drought tolerant, especially if given a mulch to help retain moisture.

Division is not required but can be done every few years in spring or summer to propagate new plants.

Tips

Hostas make wonderful woodland plants and look very attractive when combined with ferns and other fine-textured plants. Hostas are also good plants for a mixed border, particularly when used to hide the ugly, leggy lower stems and branches of some shrubs. Hostas' dense growth and thick, shade-providing leaves make them good for suppressing weeds.

Recommended

Hostas have been subjected to a great deal of crossbreeding and hybridizing, resulting in hundreds of cultivars. Visit your local garden center or get a mail-order catalog to find out what's available.

H. sieboldiana 'Elegans' (above)

Some gardeners think the flowers clash with the foliage, and they remove the flower stems when they first emerge. If you find the flowers unattractive, removing them won't harm the plant.

Also called: plantain lily **Features:** decorative foliage; white or purple, summer and fall flowers **Height:** 4–36" **Spread:** 6"–6' **Hardiness:** zones 3–8

Indian Pink

Spigelia

Indian pink is an easy-to-grow, underused native that fares well just about anywhere in the garden. In open woods it can form large colonies, but it is much tamer in an average garden setting.

Growing

Indian pink prefers **light shade** or **partial shade** but will tolerate full sun if the soil remains moist. The soil should be **fertile, moist** and **well drained**. Divide plants in spring.

Tips

Indian pink makes a nice addition to a sunny or shaded bed, border or woodland garden. It can be included in wildflower and native plant gardens and is a sure-fire draw for hummingbirds. Try it with white bleeding hearts, ferns and columbines for an attention-grabbing display.

Recommended

S. marilandica forms an upright clump of stems and foliage that remains dark green until frost. The flowers look like deep cherry red trumpets with chartreuse yellow throats. People can't help but stop to see what this gorgeous bloom is.

S. marilandica (above & below)

Indian pink is one of the best plants for attracting hummingbirds to the garden.

Also called: pinkroot **Features:** spring and early-summer, red and yellow bicolored flowers; attracts hummingbirds **Height:** 12–24" **Spread:** 18" **Hardiness:** zones 6–9

Lily-of-the-Valley

Convallaria

C. majalis var. *rosea* (above), *C. majalis* (below)

The dainty bells of lily-of-the-valley possess a heady scent, and a bunch in a small vase can delicately scent a room. They are worth growing for their timeless fragrance.

Growing

Lily-of-the-valley grows well in any light from **full sun to full shade**. The soil should be of **average fertility, humus rich** and **moist**, but all conditions are tolerated. This plant is drought resistant.

A few plants potted up in fall can be kept in a cold place for a couple of months and then brought indoors for forcing, providing you with an early touch of spring.

Tips

This versatile plant can be grown in a variety of locations. It is a good plant to naturalize in woodland gardens, perhaps bordering a pathway or beneath shade trees where little else will grow. It also makes a good groundcover in a shrub border, where its dense growth will keep the weeds down, but its shallow roots won't interfere with those of most shrubs.

Recommended

C. majalis forms a mat of foliage. In spring it produces small, arching stems lined with fragrant, white, bell-shaped flowers. **Var. *rosea*** ('Rosea') has light pink or pink-veined flowers and is less vigorous than the species.

Features: dense mat of lance-shaped foliage; white or pink, fragrant, spring flowers
Height: 6–10" **Spread:** indefinite
Hardiness: zones 2–7

Oriental Poppy
Papaver

Bold and graceful with its papery petals fluttering in the slightest breeze, Oriental poppy never fails to draw the eye.

Growing

Oriental poppies grow best in **full sun**. The soil should be **average to fertile** and **well drained**. Plants die back over the hottest part of summer, but sometimes sprout new growth in late summer or fall.

Tips

Small groups of Oriental poppies look attractive in an early-summer border, although they may leave a bare spot during their summer dormancy unless you pop in an annual or two. Baby's breath and catmint make good companions and are happy to hide your napping plant.

Recommended

P. orientale forms a basal rosette of bristly foliage and an upright clump of leafy stems. Red, scarlet, orange, pink, salmon or white flowers with prominent black stamens are borne in late spring and early summer, followed by showy seedpods. There are numerous cultivars available.

P. orientale 'Princess Victoria Louise' (above)
P. orientale (below)

This is just one of many interesting and beautiful poppies. Make a bed of annual and perennial selections for a real spring show.

Features: clump of bristly foliage; spring and early-summer flowers in shades of red, scarlet, orange, pink, salmon or white; decorative seed pods **Height:** 18"–4' **Spread:** 24–36"
Hardiness: zones 3–7

Perennial Salvia

Salvia

S. greggii cultivar (above & below)

Perennial salvias are attractive plants for the border. Taller species and cultivars add volume to the back of the border, and the smaller selections make attractive edging or feature plants near the front of the border.

Recommended

S. azurea* var. *grandiflora (blue sage) is a tall, bushy, woody perennial with gray-green foliage. It bears spikes of bright sky blue flowers in summer and fall. (Zones 5–9)

S. greggii (autumn sage) is a bushy, evergreen perennial with leathery, green leaves. It bears flowers in shades of red, pink, purple or yellow in late summer and fall. (Zones 6–10)

Perennial salvias are low-care plants that produce an abundance of flowers that attract bees, butterflies and hummingbirds.

Growing

Perennial salvias grow best in **full sun** but will tolerate light shade. The soil should be of **average fertility** and **well drained**. These plants benefit from a light mulch of compost each year and are drought tolerant once established. Deadhead to prolong blooming and trim plants back in spring to keep them looking neat.

S. 'Maraschino' (maraschino cherry sage) is a bushy hybrid sage with narrow, green leaves. It bears bright red flowers in spring, sporadically through summer and again in fall. It is one of the few red-flowered salvias hardy in New Jersey. (Zones 6–10)

The genus name Salvia *comes from the Latin* salvus, *"save," referring to the medicinal properties of several species.*

Also called: sage **Features:** woody perennial with gray-green through green foliage; spring, summer or fall flowers in shades of blue, purple, red, pink or yellow
Height: 24–36" **Spread:** 12–36"
Hardiness: zones 5–10

Primrose

Primula

These bright, cheerful harbingers of spring do wonderfully in cool weather and are among the first flowers to become available in garden centers in late winter.

Growing

Primroses grow best in **light shade** or **partial shade**. The soil should be **moderately fertile, humus rich, neutral to slightly acidic, moist** and **well drained**. Water regularly to prevent wilting and to prolong blooming. Divide after flowering or in early fall when clumps become overgrown. Many will re-seed.

Tips

Primroses make lovely additions to lightly shaded borders or even sunny borders if they are grown beneath shrubby or taller companions. They can also be included in woodland gardens, where they look good in small groups or mass-planted.

Recommended

P. denticulata (drumstick primrose, Himalayan primrose) forms a rosette of spoon-shaped leaves that are powdery white on the undersides. The early- to late-spring flowers are borne in dense, ball-like clusters atop thick stems.

P. denticulata (above & below)

P. vulgaris (common primrose, English primrose) forms a rosette of deeply veined, evergreen to semi-evergreen leaves. Clusters of flowers in shades of yellow are produced in spring.

Common primrose flowers can be made into wine or candied as edible decorations for cakes and other desserts.

Features: yellow, purple, white, pink or red, often yellow-centered, spring flowers
Height: 6–18" **Spread:** 8–12"
Hardiness: zones 4–8

Russian Sage

Perovskia

P. atriplicifolia (above), P. atriplicifolia 'Filigran' (below)

Russian sage offers four-season interest in the garden: soft, gray-green leaves on light gray stems in spring; fuzzy, violet blue flowers in summer; and silvery white stems in fall that last until late winter.

Growing

Russian sage prefers **full sun**. The soil should be of **poor to average fertility** and **well drained**. Too much water and nitrogen will cause this plant's growth to flop, so do not plant it next to heavy feeders.

Russian sage blossoms make a lovely addition to fresh bouquets and dried-flower arrangements.

In spring, when new growth appears low on the branches, or in fall, cut the plant back hard to about 6–12" to encourage vigorous, bushy growth. Russian sage cannot be divided because it is a sub-shrub that originates from a single stem.

Tips

The silvery foliage and blue flowers work well with other plants in the back of a mixed border and soften the appearance of daylilies. Russian sage can also create a soft screen in a natural garden or on a dry bank.

Recommended

P. atriplicifolia is a loose, upright plant with silvery white, finely divided foliage. The small, lavender blue flowers are loosely held on silvery, branched stems. Cultivars are available.

Features: blue or purple, mid-summer to fall flowers; attractive habit; fragrant, gray-green foliage **Height:** 3–4' **Spread:** 3–4' **Hardiness:** zones 4–9

Sedum

Sedum

S. 'Autumn Joy' (above & below)

Some 300 to 500 species of *Sedum* are distributed throughout the Northern Hemisphere. Sedums are grown for their foliage, which can range in color from steel gray-blue and green to red and burgundy, and for their flowers, which come in a wide range of colors.

Growing

Sedums prefer **full sun** but tolerate partial shade. The soil should be of **average fertility, neutral to alkaline** and very **well drained**. Over-feeding produces weak stems that will flop over. Divide in spring when needed.

Tips

Sedums give a lovely late-season display in a bed or border. The fleshy foliage stays fresh and green all summer. The flowers may take more than a month to mature from bud to flower, providing a progressive display of color the entire time.

Recommended

S. 'Autumn Joy' (autumn joy sedum) is a popular upright hybrid. The flowers open pink or red and later fade to deep bronze.

S. *spectabile* (showy stonecrop) is an upright species with pink flowers. Cultivars are available.

Also called: stonecrop Features: red, pink or white, summer to fall flowers; decorative, fleshy foliage Height: 18–24" Spread: about 24" Hardiness: zones 3–8

Teaberry

Gaultheria

G. procumbens (above & below)

This woodlander is a pretty, fragrant plant, native to eastern North America and worth growing for the glossy foliage that contrasts nicely with the persistent, red fruit. It also makes a wonderful terrarium plant, but be sure to buy nursery-grown plants rather than dig them from the woods.

Growing

Teaberries grow best in **light shade** or **partial shade**, though full sun may be tolerated in consistently moist soils. The soil should be of **average fertility, neutral to acidic, peaty** and **moist**.

Tips

These lovely plants are at home in a moist woodland garden and can be included in a shaded border if it is moist enough.

Recommended

G. procumbens is a low, spreading plant with glossy, dark green leaves that smell of wintergreen when crushed. White or pale pink, urn-shaped flowers are produced in summer and are followed by fragrant, red fruit that persists through winter.

Teaberry has a long history of herbal and medicinal use. The leaves are used for tea that is reputed to aid in breathing. The fruit is edible and has a distinctive flavor. The oil used to be used as a flavoring in toothpaste and root beer, but the flavor and is now produced synthetically.

Also called: wintergreen **Features:** glossy, dark green, wintergreen-scented foliage; white or pale pink, urn-shaped, summer flowers; persistent, aromatic, red fruit **Height:** 6–8" **Spread:** 24–36" **Hardiness:** zones 3–8

Virginia Bluebells

Mertensia

These members of the borage family emerge in early spring just as the deciduous trees are beginning to leaf out, and they bloom soon after with bright pink buds breaking into sky blue flowers.

Growing

Virginia bluebells grow best in **light shade**. The soil should be of **average fertility, humus rich, moist** and **well drained**. Plants will self-seed in good growing conditions. They go dormant in summer and can be divided at that time or in spring, just as new growth begins.

Tips

Include Virginia bluebells in a shaded border or moist woodland garden. They look wonderful inter-planted with daffodils for a lovely contrast of color.

Recommended

M. virginica forms an upright clump with blue-green leaves. It bears clusters of blue or purple-blue flowers that open from pink buds in spring.

Try not to forget where you planted these woodland perennials so that you don't dig them up by accident. They go dormant over summer and won't reappear until the following spring.

M. virginica (above & below)

Also called: Virginia cowslip **Features:** blue or purple-blue, spring flowers **Height:** 12–24" **Spread:** 10–18" **Hardiness:** zones 3–7

Yarrow

Achillea

The blooms of yarrow are some of the best to dry for flower arrangements. Yarrows are informal, tough plants with a fantastic color range.

Growing

Yarrows grow best in **full sun**. The soil should be of **average fertility, sandy** and **well drained**. These plants tolerate drought and poor soil. They will also tolerate heavy, wet soil and humidity, but they do not thrive in such conditions. Excessively rich soil or too much nitrogen results in weak, floppy growth.

Deadhead to prolong blooming; the spent flowers can be kept for dry arrangements. Basal foliage should be left in place over winter and tidied up in spring. Divide every two to three years in spring.

A. millefolium 'Paprika' (above)
A. filipendulina (below)

Yarrows make excellent groundcovers. They send up shoots and flowers from a low basal point and may be mowed periodically without excessive damage to the plant. Mower blades should be kept at least 4" high

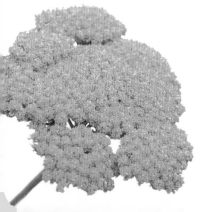

Tips

Cottage gardens, wildflower gardens and mixed borders are perfect places for these informal plants. They thrive in hot, dry locations where nothing else will grow.

Recommended

A. filipendulina forms a clump of ferny foliage and bears yellow flowers. It has been used to develop several hybrids and cultivars.

A. millefolium (common yarrow) forms a clump of soft, finely divided foliage and bears white flowers. Many cultivars exist, with flowers in a wide range of colors.

Features: white, yellow, red, orange, pink or purple, mid-summer to early-fall flowers; attractive foliage; spreading habit **Height:** 4"–4' **Spread:** 12–36" **Hardiness:** zones 3–9

Arborvitae

Thuja

*A*rborvitae are rot resistant, durable and long-lived, earning quiet admiration from gardeners everywhere. They truly live up to their name "tree of life."

Growing

Arborvitae prefer **full sun** but tolerate partial to light shade. The soil should be of **average fertility, moist** and **well drained**. These plants enjoy humidity and in the wild are often found growing near marshy areas. Arborvitae will perform best in a location with some shelter from wind, especially in winter when the foliage can easily dry out and give the entire plant a rather brown, drab appearance.

Tips

Large varieties of arborvitae make excellent specimen trees, and smaller cultivars can be used in foundation plantings and shrub borders, as formal or informal hedges and as screening plants.

Recommended

T. occidentalis (eastern arborvitae, eastern white cedar) is a narrow, pyramidal tree with scale-like, evergreen needles. There are dozens of cultivars available, including shrubby dwarf varieties, yellow-foliaged varieties and small upright varieties. **'Green Giant'** is a fast-growing selection that can grow almost 5' per year when given ample moisture. (Zones 2–7; cultivars may be less cold hardy)

T. occidentalis cultivar (above), *T. occidentalis* (below)

T. plicata (western arborvitae, western red cedar) is a narrowly pyramidal, evergreen tree that grows quickly, resists deer browsing and maintains good foliage color all winter. Several cultivars are available, including several dwarf varieties and a yellow and green variegated variety. (Zones 5–9)

Also called: cedar, tree of life
Features: small to large, evergreen shrub or tree; foliage; bark; form **Height:** 2–50'
Spread: 2–20' **Hardiness:** zones 2–9

Bayberry
Myrica

M. pensylvanica (above)

Bayberry is a fragrant shrub that can stand alone as a specimen or blend easily into a mixed border. Its aromatic, gray berries are used in the famed bayberry candles and are also loved by birds.

Growing

Bayberry grows well in **full sun** or **partial shade**. It adapts to most soil conditions from poor sandy soil to heavy clay soil. Bayberry tolerates salty conditions, making it useful where coastal conditions or winter road spray may kill less-tolerant plants. It rarely needs any pruning.

The waxy fruit of this eastern North American native has long been used in legendary candle making. Bouquets of bayberry make lovely winter decorations, especially at holiday time.

Tips

This adaptable plant forms large colonies and is often spread by birds. Its shiny, semi-evergreen foliage is quite handsome when used for mass plantings in areas with poor soil and in seaside gardens.

Recommended

M. pensylvanica is a dense, rounded, suckering shrub with insignificant flowers that are borne in early to midspring. Male and female flowers are generally produced on separate plants, but sometimes the plants are monoecious. Both male and female plants are required for a good show of fruit on the female. Small, waxy, gray berries persist through winter.

Features: aromatic, deciduous to semi-evergreen shrub; attractive foliage; dense, suckering habit; persistent fruit
Height: 5–12' **Spread:** 5–12'
Hardiness: zones 3–6

Beech
Fagus

The aristocrats of the large shade trees, majestic beeches are attractive at any age, from their big, bold, beautiful youth through to their slow, craggy decline.

Growing
Beeches grow equally well in **full sun** or **partial shade**. The soil should be of **average fertility, loamy** and **well drained**, though almost all well-drained soils are tolerated.

American beech doesn't like having its roots disturbed and should be transplanted only when very young. European beech transplants easily and is more tolerant of varied soil conditions than is American beech.

Tips
Beeches make excellent specimens. They are also used as shade trees and in woodland gardens. These trees need a lot of space, but European beech's adaptability to pruning makes it a reasonable choice in a small garden where the gardener is able to prune it.

Recommended
F. grandifolia (American beech) is a broad-canopied tree native to most of eastern North America.

F. sylvatica (European beech) is a spectacular, broad tree with a number of interesting cultivars. Several are small enough to use in the home

F. grandifolia (above), *F. sylvatica* (below)

garden, from narrow columnar and weeping varieties to varieties with purple or yellow leaves or pink, white and green variegated foliage.

The nuts of beech trees are edible when roasted. These are the trees of legends, magnificent specimens that last for many generations.

Features: large, oval, deciduous shade tree; foliage; bark; habit; fall color; fruit
Height: 30–80' **Spread:** 10–65'
Hardiness: zones 4–9

Caryopteris
Caryopteris

Caryopteris is cultivated for its aromatic stems, foliage and blue flowers. A few cut stems in a vase will fill a room with their delicate scent. A shrub in the garden is often a butterfly magnet.

Growing
Caryopteris prefers **full sun** but tolerates light shade. It does best in soil of **average fertility** that is **light** and **well drained**. Wet and poorly drained soils can kill this plant. Caryopteris is very drought tolerant once established. Treat it as an herbaceous perennial if growth is regularly killed back over winter, but wait until spring to cut it back.

Tips
Include caryopteris in your shrub or mixed border. The bright blue, late-season flowers are welcome when many other plants are past their flowering best.

Recommended
C. x *clandonensis* forms a dense mound up to 3' tall and 3–5' in spread. It bears clusters of blue or purple flowers in late summer and early fall. Cultivars are available and are more often grown than the species.

Caryopteris is sometimes killed back over cold winters. Cut back the dead growth in spring and give a generous handful of time-release fertilizer. New shoots will sprout from the base, providing you with plenty of late-summer flowers.

C. x *clandonensis* cultivar (above)
C. x *clandonensis* (below)

Also called: bluebeard, blue spirea
Features: rounded, spreading, deciduous shrub with attractive, fragrant foliage, twigs and late-summer flowers **Height:** 2–4'
Spread: 2–5' **Hardiness:** zones 5–9

Chokeberry
Aronia

A. melanocarpa cultivar (above), A. melanocarpa (below)

These lovely shrubs deserve to be more widely planted. With clusters of white flowers in spring, glossy foliage that turns orange and red in fall and decorative fruit that persists all winter, chokeberries have something to offer year-round.

Growing

Chokeberries grow well in **full sun** or **partial shade,** with best flowering and fruiting in full sun. The soil should be of **average fertility** and **well drained**, although the plants adapt to most soil conditions. Wet, dry or poor soil conditions are tolerated.

Tips

Chokeberries are useful shrubs to include in shrub and natural borders, and they make interesting, low-maintenance specimen plants. Left to their own devices, they can colonize a fairly large area.

Recommended

A. arbutifolia (red chokeberry) is an upright shrub that bears white flowers in late spring and bright red, waxy fruit in fall. The glossy, dark green foliage turns red in fall. Cultivars are available.

A. melanocarpa (black chokeberry) is an upright, suckering shrub native to the eastern U.S. The white flowers of late spring are followed by black fruit in fall. The glossy, green foliage turns bright red to purple in fall. Cultivars are available.

Also called: aronia **Features:** suckering, deciduous shrub; attractive, white, spring flowers; fall fruit; colorful fall foliage **Height:** 3–6' **Spread:** 3–10' **Hardiness:** zones 3–8

Crape Myrtle
Lagerstroemia

L. indica cultivar (both photos)

Loose clusters of colorful, ruffled flowers can cover this attractive, small tree from early summer to fall.

Growing
Crape myrtle prefers **full sun** and tolerates light shade. The soil should be of **average fertility, neutral to slightly acidic** and **well drained**. Established plants are fairly drought tolerant but benefit from deep watering during periods of extended drought. Avoid wetting the foliage to reduce the incidence of powdery mildew.

Tips
These small trees make lovely specimen plants and provide light shade in a border. Low-growing, shrubby selections can be used in shrub and mixed borders and for hedging and screening.

Recommended
L. indica is a small, multi-stemmed tree or large shrub. It has peeling bark and dark green leaves that are bronzy when they emerge in spring and turn shades of yellow, orange or red in fall. Clusters of flowers in shades of pink, red, purple or white are produced from summer through fall. Choose mildew-resistant cultivars. Tall and dwarf selections are available.

The trees are especially showy in the historic seaside town of Cape May, New Jersey, where they adorn many of the Victorian mansions that line the streets. Their fall color is outstanding.

Features: multi-stemmed, deciduous tree or shrub; early-summer through fall flowers in shades of pink, red, purple or white; exfoliating bark; fall color **Height:** 3–25' **Spread:** 3–25' **Hardiness:** zones 7–9

Cryptomeria
Cryptomeria

This unique evergreen is perhaps best described as fluffy and puffy. It is fast growing and demands a place of prominence in the garden.

Growing
Cryptomeria grows well in **full sun** or **partial shade**. The soil should be **fertile, humus rich, moist** and **well drained**, though plants adapt to a wide range of soil conditions. Mulch plants well to retain moisture during periods of extended drought.

Tips
Cryptomeria makes an interesting specimen tree, though it is too large for a small garden. The dwarf cultivars are an excellent choice for mixed beds and borders and can be used as screening plants.

Recommended
C. japonica is a conical to columnar, evergreen conifer with pendulous sprays of needles. The blue-green color turns bronzy or brown in winter. Dwarf cultivars are available as well as cultivars that stay green over winter and that have interesting crested or twisted needles.

These trees can live for thousands of years! Many ancient stands can be seen in Asia, where the wood is used because it is strong, rot resistant and workable.

C. japonica (above), C. japonica 'Radicans' (below)

Features: conical to columnar evergreen; attractive needles; fall color **Height:** 1–80'
Spread: 1–25' **Hardiness:** zones 6–8

Dawn Redwood

Metasequoia

M. glyptostroboides 'Ogon' (above)
M. glyptostroboides (below)

This stunning tree, once known only from the fossil record, has found well-deserved acclaim and popularity since its re-introduction to North America.

Growing

Dawn redwood grows well in **full sun** or **light shade**. The soil should be **humus rich, slightly acidic, moist** and **well drained**. Wet and dry soils are tolerated, though growth is reduced in dry conditions. This tree likes the humid conditions found in New Jersey. Mulch and water regularly until it is established.

Tips

This large tree needs plenty of room to grow. Large gardens and parks can best accommodate it. As a single specimen or in a group planting, dawn redwood looks attractive and impressive. The buttressing of the trunk will occur only if the lower branches are left in place.

Recommended

M. glyptostroboides has a pyramidal, sometimes spire-like form. The tree's needles turn gold or orange in fall before dropping. Cultivars are available but do not differ significantly from the species.

It is fun to grow this giant in New Jersey, where it becomes a real conversation piece.

Features: narrow, conical, deciduous conifer; soft green foliage turns gold to orange in fall; buttressed trunk **Height:** 70–125' **Spread:** 15–25' **Hardiness:** zones 4–8

Dogwood
Cornus

Color, habit, adaptability and hardiness are all positive attributes to be found in dogwoods.

Growing

Dogwoods grow well in **full sun, light shade** or **partial shade**, with a slight preference for light shade. The soil should be of **average to high fertility, high in organic matter, neutral to slightly acidic** and **well drained**.

Tips

Shrub dogwoods look best in groups. The tree species make wonderful specimen plants and are small enough to include in most gardens. Use them along the edge of a woodland, in a shrub or mixed border, alongside a house or near a pond, water feature or patio.

Recommended

C. alba (red-twig dogwood, Tartarian dogwood), *C. sericea* (*C. stolonifera*; red-osier dogwood) and their cultivars are grown for their bright red, orange or yellow stems that provide winter interest and for their fall foliage color. (Zones 2–7)

C. alternifolia (pagoda dogwood) can be grown as a large, multi-stemmed shrub or a small, single-stemmed tree. The branches have an attractive layered appearance. It bears clusters of small, white flowers in early summer. (Zones 3–8)

C. florida (flowering dogwood) is a small tree with horizontally layered

C. alba 'Bailhalo' (above), *C. kousa* var. *chinensis* (below)

branches and late-spring flowers with pink or white bracts. (Zones 5–9)

C. kousa (Kousa dogwood) is grown for its white-bracted flowers, red fall fruit, red and purple fall color and interesting bark. **Var. *chinensis*** (Chinese dogwood) grows more vigorously and has larger flowers. Both are often used in place of the native *C. florida* in southern New Jersey because they are more disease resistant. (Zones 5–9)

Features: deciduous large shrub or small tree; late-spring to early-summer flowers; fall foliage; stem color; fruit; habit **Height:** 5–30' **Spread:** 5–30' **Hardiness:** zones 2–9

Enkianthus
Enkianthus

E. campanulatus (above & below)

The layered branching and tufted foliage of enkianthus will add a unique touch to your garden. Blooms occur on the previous year's growth, so any pruning should be done immediately after flowering.

This plant is one of the best shrubs for adding stunning fall color to your garden.

Growing
Enkianthus grows well in **full sun, partial shade** or **light shade**. The soil should be **fertile, humus rich, moist, acidic** and **well drained**.

Tips
Enkianthus is a beautiful shrub to include in the understory of a woodland garden and can be used in a mixed border or as a specimen plant. It also makes an excellent companion for rhododendrons and other acid-loving plants.

Recommended
E. campanulatus (red-vein enkianthus) is a large, bushy shrub or small tree that grows 10–15' tall with an equal spread. It bears clusters of small, white, red-veined, pendulous, bell-shaped flowers in spring. Its foliage turns fantastic shades of yellow, orange and red in fall. (Zones 4–7)

E. perulatus (white enkianthus) is a compact shrub that grows 5–6' tall with an equal spread. It produces white flowers in mid-spring. Its foliage turns bright red in fall. (Zones 5–8)

Features: bushy, deciduous shrub or small tree; spring flowers; fall foliage **Height:** 5–15' **Spread:** 5–15' **Hardiness:** zones 4–8

False Cypress
Chamaecyparis

C. obtusa 'Nana Gracilis' (above), *C. pisifera* 'Filifera Aurea' (below)

Conifer shoppers are blessed with a marvelous selection of false cypresses that offer color, size, shape and growth habits not available in most other evergreens.

Growing
False cypresses prefer **full sun**. The soil should be **fertile, moist, neutral to acidic** and **well drained**. Alkaline soils are tolerated. In shaded areas, growth may be sparse or thin.

Tips
Tree varieties are used as specimen plants and for hedging. Dwarf and slow-growing cultivars are used in borders and rock gardens and as bonsai. False cypress shrubs can be grown near the house or as evergreen specimens in large containers.

Recommended
There are several available species of false cypress as well as many cultivars. The scaly foliage can be in a drooping or strand form, in fan-like or feathery sprays and may be dark green, bright green or yellow. Plant forms vary too, from mounding or rounded to tall and pyramidal or narrow with pendulous branches. Check with your local garden center or nursery to see what is available.

The oils in the foliage of false cypresses may be irritating to sensitive skin.

Features: narrow, pyramidal, evergreen tree or shrub; cultivars vary; foliage; habit; cones
Height: 18"–150' **Spread:** 18"–80'
Hardiness: zones 4–8

Flowering Cherry, Plum & Almond

Prunus

P. sargentii (above), P. x cistena (below)

Cherries are so beautiful and uplift-ing after the gray days of winter that few gardeners can resist them.

Growing

These flowering fruit trees prefer **full sun**. The soil should be of **average fertility, moist** and **well drained.** Shallow roots will emerge from the lawn if the tree is not getting

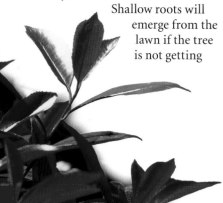

sufficient water. They will not tolerate soil with poor drainage.

Tips

Prunus species are beautiful as specimen plants, and many are small enough to be included in almost any garden. Small species and cultivars can also be included in borders or grouped to form informal hedges or barriers. Pissard plum and purple leaf sand cherry can be trained into formal hedges.

Pest problems make many cherries rather short-lived. Choose resistant species such as Sargent cherry. If you plant a more susceptible species, such as Japanese flowering cherry, enjoy it while it thrives but be prepared to replace it.

Recommended

Following are a few popular selections from the many species, hybrids and cultivars available. **P. cerasifera 'Atropurpurea'** (Pissard plum) and **P. x cistena** (purple leaf sand cherry) are shrubby plants grown for their purple foliage and light pink flowers. **P. sargentii** (Sargent cherry) and **P. serrulata** (Japanese flowering cherry) are rounded or spreading trees grown for their white or light pink flowers as well as their attractive bark and bright fall color.

Features: upright, rounded, spreading or weeping, deciduous tree or shrub; spring to early-summer flowers; fruit; bark; fall foliage
Height: 4–75' **Spread:** 4–50'
Hardiness: zones 4–8

Fothergilla
Fothergilla

F. gardenii 'Blue Mist' (above), *F. major* (below)

Flowers, fragrance, fall color and interesting, soft tan to brownish stems give fothergillas year-round appeal.

Growing

Fothergillas grow equally well in **full sun** or **partial shade**. In full sun these plants bear the most flowers, but a bit of shade in the warmest part of the day will extend the blooming period. The soil should be of **average fertility, acidic, humus rich, moist** and **well drained**.

Tips

Fothergillas are attractive and useful in shrub or mixed borders, in woodland gardens and when combined with evergreen groundcover. The fall color is outstanding.

Recommended

F. gardenii (dwarf fothergilla) is a bushy shrub that bears fragrant, white flowers. The foliage turns yellow, orange and red in fall. Cultivars are available.

F. major (large fothergilla) is a large, rounded shrub that bears fragrant, white flowers. The fall colors are yellow, orange and scarlet. Cultivars are available.

The fuzzy, bottlebrush-shaped flowers of fothergillas have a delicate honey scent.

Features: dense, rounded or bushy, deciduous shrub; spring flowers; scent; fall foliage
Height: 2–10' **Spread:** 2–10'
Hardiness: zones 4–9

Franklinia
Franklinia

F. alatamaha (above & below)

This plant is a beautiful, small tree that offers lovely, mid- to late-summer flowers and glorious, bright red or reddish purple fall color. Its gray bark is evident in winter.

Growing
Franklinias grow well in **full sun** or **partial shade**, with the best flower production and fall color occurring in full sun. The soil should be of **average fertility, humus rich, neutral to acidic, moist** and **well drained**.

Tips
Franklinias are diminutive enough to be suitable in almost all gardens. In a small garden they can be used as shade trees, while in a larger garden they may be used as specimen trees or to provide light shade in a mixed or shrub border.

Recommended
F. alatamaha is a small, upright tree with spreading branches that create an attractive, open appearance. It bears fragrant, white, cup-shaped flowers in mid- to late summer. Its leaves turn brilliant red in fall.

This tree was discovered growing on the banks of the Alatamaha River in Georgia by John Bertram in 1770, but there are believed to be no remaining wild specimens, as the tree was only found in the wild on two other documented occasions.

Also called: Franklin tree **Features:** deciduous tree with an upright, open habit; late-summer flowers; fall color **Height:** 10–20' **Spread:** 6–15' **Hardiness:** zones 5–8

Fringe Tree
Chionanthus

C. virginicus (above & below)

Fringe trees adapt to a wide range of growing conditions, are cold hardy and are densely covered in silky, white, honey-scented flowers that shimmer in the wind over a long period in spring.

Growing

Fringe trees prefer **full sun**. They do best in soil that is **fertile, acidic, moist** and **well drained** but will adapt to most soil conditions. In the wild they are often found growing alongside stream banks.

Tips

Fringe trees work well as specimen plants, as part of a border or beside a water feature. Plants begin flowering at a very early age.

Features: rounded or spreading, deciduous large shrub or small tree; early-summer flowers; bark; habit **Height:** 10–25' **Spread:** 10–25' **Hardiness:** zones 4–9

Recommended

C. retusus (Chinese fringe tree) is a rounded, spreading shrub or small tree with deeply furrowed, peeling bark and erect, fragrant, white flower clusters. (Zones 5–8)

C. virginicus (white fringe tree) is a spreading small tree or large shrub that bears drooping, fragrant, white flowers. (Zones 4–8)

Holly
Ilex

I. x meserveae cultivar (above)
I. x meserveae 'Blue Girl' (below)

Hollies vary greatly in shape and size. They are a natural in New Jersey and very beneficial in attracting birds because the berries are a food source and the leaves offer protection.

Growing
These plants prefer **full sun** but tolerate partial shade. The soil should be of **average to rich fertility, humus rich, acidic** and **moist**. Shelter from winter wind to help prevent evergreen

leaves from drying out is beneficial. Apply a summer mulch to keep the roots cool and moist.

Tips
Hollies can be used in groups, in woodland gardens and in shrub and mixed borders. They can also be shaped into hedges. Winterberry is good for naturalizing in moist sites in the garden.

Recommended
I. x attenuata 'Fosteri' (Foster's holly) is a pyramidal holly with glossy, green foliage and bright red fruit. (Zones 6–9)

I. x meserveae (meserve holly, blue holly) is a group of hybrids that originated from crosses between tender English holly (*I. aquifolium*) and hardy hollies like prostrate holly (*I. rugosa*). These dense, evergreen shrubs may be erect, mounding or spreading. (Zones 5–8)

I. 'Sparkleberry' is a deciduous, upright female hybrid that bears lots of glossy, red fruit that persists well into winter. It was developed from a cross between *I. verticillata* and *I. serrata*.

I. verticillata (winterberry, winter-berry holly) is a deciduous native species grown for its explosion of red fruit that persists into winter. Many cultivars and hybrids are available.

Also called: inkberry, winterberry
Features: erect or spreading, evergreen or deciduous shrub or tree; glossy, sometimes spiny foliage; fruit; habit **Height:** 3–50'
Spread: 3–40' **Hardiness:** zones 3–9

Horse Chestnut
Aesculus

A. parviflora (above), A. hippocastanum (below)

Horse chestnuts range from trees with immense regal bearing to small but impressive shrubs. All have spectacular flowers.

Growing

Horse chestnuts grow well in **full sun** or **partial shade**. The soil should be **fertile, moist** and **well drained**. These trees dislike excessive drought.

Tips

Horse chestnuts are used as specimen and shade trees. The roots of horse chestnuts can break up sidewalks and patios if planted too close.

The smaller, shrubby horse chestnuts grow well near pond plantings and also make interesting specimens. Give them plenty of space, as they can form large colonies.

Recommended

A. hippocastanum (common horse chestnut) is a large, rounded tree that will branch right to the ground if grown in an open setting. The flowers, white with yellow or pink marks, are borne in long spikes. (Zones 3–7)

A. parviflora (bottlebrush buckeye) is a spreading, mound-forming, suckering shrub that has plentiful spikes of creamy white flowers. (Zones 4–9)

A. pavia (red buckeye) is a low-growing to rounded, shrubby tree with cherry red flowers and handsome foliage. It needs consistent moisture. (Zones 4–8)

Also called: buckeye **Features:** rounded or spreading, deciduous tree or shrub; early-summer flowers; foliage; spiny fruit
Height: 8–80' **Spread:** 8–65'
Hardiness: zones 3–9

Hydrangea

Hydrangea

H. *quercifolia* (above)
H. *macrophylla* cultivar (below)

Hydrangeas have showy, long-lasting flowers and glossy, green leaves, some of which turn beautiful colors in fall.

Growing

Hydrangeas grow well in **full sun** or **partial shade**, and most species tolerate full shade. Some shade will reduce leaf and flower scorch in hotter gardens. The soil should

be of **average to high fertility, humus rich, moist** and **well drained**. As their name suggests, these plants need a lot of water.

Tips

Hydrangeas come in many forms and have many uses in the landscape. They can be included in shrub or mixed borders, used as specimens or informal barriers and planted in groups or containers.

Recommended

H. arborescens (smooth hydrangea) is a rounded shrub that flowers well even in shady conditions. This species is rarely grown in favor of the cultivars that bear large clusters of showy, white blossoms.

H. macrophylla (big leaf hydrangea) is a rounded shrub that bears flowers in shades of pink, red, blue or purple from mid- to late summer. Many cultivars are available. (Zones 5–9)

H. paniculata (panicle hydrangea) is a spreading to upright large shrub or small tree that bears white flowers from late summer to early fall. 'Grandiflora' (Peegee hydrangea) is a commonly available cultivar. (Zones 4–8)

H. quercifolia (oakleaf hydrangea) is a mound-forming shrub with attractive, cinnamon brown, exfoliating bark. The large, dramatic, conical clusters of sterile and fertile flowers are long lasting. (Zones 4–8)

Features: deciduous; mounding or spreading shrub or tree; flowers; habit; foliage; bark
Height: 3–20' **Spread:** 3–10'
Hardiness: zones 3–9

Juniper
Juniperus

J. horizontalis 'Blue Chip' (above), *J. horizontalis* 'Blue Prince' (below)

When nothing else will grow in a hot, dry, sunny area, try a juniper. Once established, they need little or no care and can be quite colorful and handsome.

Growing

Junipers prefer **full sun** but tolerate light shade. Ideally the soil should be of **average fertility** and **well drained**, but these plants tolerate most conditions.

Tips

There are endless uses for junipers in the garden. They make prickly barriers and hedges and can be used in borders, as specimens or in groups. The larger species can be used to form windbreaks, while the low-growing species can be used in rock gardens and as groundcovers. Junipers both feed and shelter songbirds.

Recommended

Junipers vary from species to species, and often within a species. Cultivars are available and may differ significantly from the species. *J. chinensis* (Chinese juniper) is a conical tree or spreading shrub. *J. horizontalis* (creeping juniper) is a prostrate, creeping groundcover. *J. procumbens* (Japanese garden juniper) is a wide-spreading, stiff-branched, low shrub. *J. scopulorum* (Rocky Mountain juniper) can be upright, rounded, weeping or spreading. *J. squamata* (single seed juniper) forms a prostrate or low, spreading shrub or a small, upright tree. *J. virginiana* (eastern red cedar) is a durable, upright or wide-spreading, native tree.

Features: conical or columnar tree or rounded or spreading shrub or prostrate groundcover; evergreen; foliage; variety of colors, sizes and habits **Height:** 4"–80'
Spread: 18"–25' **Hardiness:** zones 3–9

Katsura-Tree

Cercidiphyllum

C. japonicum 'Pendula' (above)
C. japonicum (below)

Katsura-tree is native to eastern Asia, and its delicate foliage blends well in Japanese-style gardens.

Katsura-tree adds distinction and grace to the garden. Even in youth it is poised and elegant, and it is bound to become a bewitching mature specimen.

Growing

Katsura-tree grows equally well in **full sun** or **partial shade**. The soil should be **fertile, humus rich, neutral to acidic, moist** and **well drained**. It is very important to water well during dry spells for the first couple of years to help this tree establish more quickly.

Tips

Katsura-tree is useful as a specimen or shade tree. The species is quite large and is best used in large gardens. The cultivar 'Pendula,' although it spreads quite wide, can be used in smaller gardens.

Recommended

C. japonicum is a slow-growing tree with heart-shaped, blue-green leaves that turn yellow and orange in fall and develop a spicy fragrance. **'Pendula'** is one of the most elegant weeping trees available. When grafted to a standard, the mounding, cascading branches give the entire tree the appearance of a waterfall tumbling over rocks.

Features: rounded, spreading or weeping, often multi-stemmed, deciduous tree; attractive foliage; fall color **Height:** 10–65' **Spread:** 10–65' **Hardiness:** zones 4–8

Lilac

Syringa

The hardest thing about growing lilacs is choosing from the many species and hundreds of cultivars available.

Growing

Lilacs grow best in **full sun**. The soil should be **fertile, humus rich** and **well drained**. Add a cup or so of lime early each spring. These plants tolerate open, windy locations.

Tips

Include lilacs in a shrub or mixed border or use them to create an informal hedge. Japanese tree lilac can be used as a specimen tree.

Recommended

S. x *hyacinthiflora* (hyacinth-flowered lilac, early-flowering lilac) is a group of hardy, upright hybrids that become spreading as they mature. Clusters of fragrant flowers appear two weeks earlier than those of the French lilacs. The leaves turn reddish purple in fall. Many cultivars are available. (Zones 3–7)

S. meyeri (Meyer lilac) is a compact, rounded shrub that bears pink or lavender, fragrant flowers. (Zones 3–7)

S. reticulata (Japanese tree lilac) is a rounded large shrub or small tree that bears white flowers. **'Ivory Silk'** has a more compact habit and produces more flowers than the species. (Zones 3–7)

S. vulgaris (French lilac, common lilac) is the plant most people think

S. meyeri (above), *S. vulgaris* (below)

of when they think of lilacs. It is a suckering, spreading shrub with an irregular habit that bears fragrant, lilac-colored flowers. Hundreds of cultivars with a variety of flower colors are available. (Zones 3–8)

Features: rounded or suckering, deciduous shrub or small tree; late-spring to mid-summer flowers; habit **Height:** 3–30' **Spread:** 3–25' **Hardiness:** zones 2–8

Linden
Tilia

T. cordata (above)

Lindens are picturesque shade trees with sweet-scented flowers that capture the essence of summer.

Growing

Lindens grow best in **full sun**. The soil should be **average to fertile, moist** and **well drained**. These trees adapt to most pH levels but prefer an **alkaline** soil. They tolerate pollution and urban conditions.

Tips

Lindens are useful and attractive street, shade and specimen trees. Their tolerance of pollution and their moderate size make lindens ideal for city gardens.

Recommended

T. cordata (little leaf linden) is a dense, pyramidal tree that may become rounded with age. It bears small, fragrant flowers with narrow, yellow-green bracts. Cultivars are available.

T. tomentosa (silver linden) has a broad, pyramidal or rounded habit. It bears small, fragrant flowers and has glossy, green leaves with fuzzy, silvery undersides.

Many countries have linden festivals in July when lindens are in bloom. Tea made from the blooms is a valuable, health-enhancing beverage.

Features: dense, pyramidal to rounded, deciduous tree; habit; foliage **Height:** 20–65' **Spread:** 15–50' **Hardiness:** zones 3–8

Magnolia
Magnolia

Magnolias are beautiful, fragrant, versatile plants that also provide attractive winter structure.

Growing

Magnolias grow well in **full sun** or **partial shade**. The soil should be **fertile, humus rich, acidic, moist** and **well drained**. Summer mulch will help keep the roots cool and the soil moist.

Tips

Magnolias are used as specimen trees, and the smaller species can be used in borders.

Avoid planting magnolias where the morning sun will encourage the blooms to open too early in the season. Cold, wind and rain can damage the blossoms.

Recommended

Many species, hybrids and cultivars, in a range of sizes and with differing flowering times and flower colors, are available. Some popular selections include **M. x *soulangeana*** (saucer magnolia), a rounded, spreading, deciduous shrub or tree with pink, purple or white flowers; **M. *stellata*** (star magnolia), a compact, bushy or spreading, deciduous shrub or small tree with many-petalled, fragrant, white flowers; and **M. *virginiana*** (swamp magnolia, sweet bay magnolia), an open, spreading shrub or

M. stellata (above), M. x soulangeana (below)

small, multi-stemmed tree that bears very fragrant, white flowers in late spring or early summer. Check with your local nursery or garden center for other available magnolias.

Features: upright to spreading, deciduous or evergreen shrub or tree; fragrant flowers; fruit; foliage; habit; bark **Height:** 8–40' **Spread:** 5–35' **Hardiness:** zones 4–9

Maple
Acer

A. palmatum cultivar (above), *A. palmatum* var. *dissectum* cultivar (below)

Maples are attractive all year, with delicate flowers in spring, attractive foliage and hanging samaras in summer, vibrant leaf color in fall and interesting bark and branch structures in winter.

Growing

Most maples do well in **full sun** or **light shade**. The soil should be **fertile, moist, high in organic matter** and **well drained**.

Tips

Maples can be used as specimen trees, as large elements in shrub or mixed borders or as hedges. Some are useful as understory plants bordering wooded areas; others can be grown in containers on patios or terraces. Few Japanese gardens are without the smaller maples. Almost all maples can be used to create bonsai specimens.

Recommended

Maples are some of the most popular shade or street trees. Many are very large when mature, but a few smaller species include **A. campestre** (hedge maple), **A. ginnala** (amur maple), **A. palmatum** (Japanese maple) and **A. palmatum** var. **dissectum** (cut-leaf Japanese maple). Check with your local nursery or garden center for availability.

Features: single- or multi-stemmed, fast-growing, deciduous shade tree or large shrub; foliage; bark; winged fruit; fall color; form; flowers **Height:** 6–80' **Spread:** 6–70' **Hardiness:** zones 3–8

Nandina
Nandina

These plants are beautiful all year long, but they really stand out in winter, when their shiny evergreen foliage glistens in the sun and the huge clusters of red berries make them a real showpiece.

Growing

Nandina grows best in **partial shade** or **light shade** in a sheltered location. The soil should be of **average fertility, moist** and **well drained**. Trim shrubs back from time to time if you want to maintain the stocky, bamboo-like appearance that gives this shrub its alternate common name.

Tips

This versatile shrub adds a touch of elegance to shrub or mixed borders, foundation plantings and water features. Grow it near doors, along pathways or in entrance beds to best appreciate it in winter. The low-growing selections can be used as groundcovers and to reduce soil erosion on banks that are too awkward to mow.

Recommended

N. domestica is an upright, evergreen or semi-evergreen shrub. New growth is red or purple tinged, maturing to glossy green and turning red or purple in winter. Conical clusters of small,

N. domestica (above), *N. domestica* 'Compacta' (below)

white, star-shaped flowers are produced in summer, followed by bright red fruit that persists into winter. The species grows 4–6' tall and 5' wide, though smaller cultivars, ranging from 18–36" tall, are available.

The large clusters of berries are wonderful decorations on evergreen wreaths or garlands and really brighten up the winter landscape. Their delicate puffs of blooms in spring add another dimension to this versatile plant.

Also called: heavenly bamboo
Features: evergreen to semi-evergreen, upright shrub; decorative foliage; white, summer flowers; bright red, persistent fruit
Height: 18"–6' **Spread:** 2–5'
Hardiness: 6–9

Needle Palm
Rhapidophyllum

R. hystrix (both photos)

Needle palm, named for the long, sharp needles found on its trunk, is the most cold-tolerant palm in the world and will thrive in New Jersey.

Growing

Needle palm grows best in **partial shade** in a sheltered location out of the winter wind. The soil should be of **average fertility, moist** and **well drained**. Needle palm is tolerant of moist sites.

Tips

Needle palm is best used as a unique specimen plant. It works well in containers where it can be used as a patio specimen and moved indoors in winter if you aren't confident of its hardiness. In a sheltered location, it adds a tropical touch to a border or entryway planting.

Recommended

R. hystrix is a low-growing, clump-forming palm. The bright green, fan-shaped leaves are deeply lobed with pointed tips and can be up to 36" long. The tiny, red or purple flowers are produced in summer and are often obscured by the foliage.

This species is becoming less common in the wild, and it is thought that an extinct sloth was the animal that ate and spread the seeds. Today, only a few animals, including black bears, eat the fruit.

Features: clump-forming palm; attractive foliage **Height:** 10–12' **Spread:** 6–12' **Hardiness:** zones 7–9

Ninebark

Physocarpus

P. opulifolius DIABOLO (above & below)

This attractive native deserves wider recognition, especially now that attractive cultivars with foliage ranging in color from yellow to purple are available. It provides great four-season interest.

Growing

Ninebark grows well in **full sun** or **partial shade**. The best leaf coloring develops in a sunny location. The soil should be **fertile, acidic, moist** and **well drained**.

Tips

Ninebark can be included in a shrub or mixed border, in a woodland garden or in a naturalistic garden.

Recommended

P. opulifolius (common ninebark) is a suckering shrub with long, arching branches and exfoliating bark. It bears light pink flowers in early summer and fruit that ripens to reddish green in fall. Several cultivars with beautifully colored foliage include **'Dart's Gold,'** DIABOLO, **'Nugget,'** and SUMMER WINE. SUMMER WINE is very compact and desirable in a small landscape.

Also called: common ninebark
Features: upright, sometimes suckering, deciduous shrub; early-summer flowers; fruit; bark; foliage **Height:** 4–10' **Spread:** 4–15'
Hardiness: zones 2–8

Oak

Quercus

Q. alba (above)

Growing

Oaks grow well in **full sun** or **partial shade**. The soil should be **fertile, moist** and **well drained**. These trees can be difficult to establish; transplant them only while they are young.

Tips

Oaks are large trees that are best as specimens or for groves in parks and large gardens. Do not disturb the ground around the base of an oak; this tree is very sensitive to changes in grade.

Recommended

There are many oaks to choose from. A few popular species are **Q. acutissima** (saw tooth oak), a rounded tree with sharply toothed, glossy, green leaves and beautiful, ornamental, egg-shaped acorns; **Q. alba** (white oak), a rounded, spreading tree with peeling bark and purple-red fall color; **Q. coccinea** (scarlet oak), noted for having the most brilliant red fall color of all the oaks; and **Q. rubra** (*Q. borealis* var. *maxima*; red oak), a rounded, spreading tree with fall color ranging from yellow to red-brown. Check with your local nursery or garden center to see what is available.

Oaks are valued for beauty, strength and posterity. Oaks have a deep, rich fall color that extends the foliage display by several weeks.

Despite their bitter kernels, acorns are eaten by deer, squirrels and birds.

Features: large, rounded, spreading, deciduous tree; summer and fall foliage; bark; habit; acorns **Height:** 35–120' **Spread:** 10–100' **Hardiness:** zones 3–9

Pine

Pinus

The Pine Barrens have some unique varieties that should be left and protected when homes are built. It is always best to use native pines if and when they are available, but there are many other pines that will do very well in New Jersey.

Growing

Pines grow best in **full sun**. These trees adapt to most **well-drained** soils but do not tolerate polluted urban conditions. Pines are not heavy feeders; fertilizing will encourage rapid new growth that is weak and susceptible to pest and disease problems.

Tips

Pines can be used as specimen trees, as hedges or to create windbreaks. Smaller cultivars can be included in shrub or mixed borders.

Recommended

P. echinata (shortleaf pine) is a broad, pyramidal tree with bright green needles and reddish brown, scaly bark. (Zones 6–9)

P. rigida (pitch pine) is a striking and beautiful, rounded to irregular native of the Pine Barrens. Often hard to find in nurseries, it should be retained by builders. (Zones 4–8)

P. strobus (white pine) is a fast-growing, slender, conical tree with soft, plumy, dark green needles. Cultivars are available. (Zones 3–8)

P. thunbergii (Japanese black pine) is a conical to rounded tree with long, gray-green needles and purple-gray

P. strobus 'Contorta' (above), *P. strobus* (below)

bark. It is tolerant of salt spray. (Zones 5–8)

P. virginiana (Virginia pine) is a small tree or large shrub with an irregular, spreading habit and often twisted branches with light to dark green needles. (Zones 5–9)

Features: upright, columnar or spreading, evergreen tree; foliage; bark; cones; habit
Height: 2–120' **Spread:** 2–60'
Hardiness: zones 2–8

Redbud
Cercis

Redbud is an exceptional treasure of spring. Deep magenta flowers bloom before the leaves emerge, and their impact is intense. As the buds open, the flowers turn pink, covering the long, thin branches in pastel clouds.

Growing
Redbud will grow well in **full sun, partial shade** or **light shade**. The soil should be a **fertile, deep loam** that is **moist** and **well drained**. This plant has tender roots and does not like being transplanted.

Tips
Redbud can be used as a specimen tree, in a shrub or mixed border or in a woodland garden. It tends to self-seed and can be short-lived.

Recommended
C. canadensis (eastern redbud) is a spreading, multi-stemmed tree that bears red, purple or pink flowers. The young foliage is bronze, fading to green over summer and turning bright yellow in fall. Many beautiful cultivars are available.

C. canadensis (above & below)

Redbuds are not as long-lived as many other trees, so use their delicate beauty to supplement more permanent trees in the garden. They look lovely dancing randomly through the spring garden, like maidens dressed for a garden party.

Features: rounded or spreading, multi-stemmed, deciduous tree or shrub; spring flowers; fall foliage **Height:** 20–30' **Spread:** 25–35' **Hardiness:** zones 4–9

Serviceberry
Amelanchier

Serviceberries are North American natives with pure white, glistening flowers that are often among the earliest to bloom in the forest or garden, followed by edible berries. The fall foliage color ranges from glowing apricot to deep red.

Growing

Serviceberries grow well in **full sun** or **light shade**. They prefer **acidic** soil that is **fertile, humus rich, moist** and **well drained**. They are often found along streams, but they can tolerate some drought.

Tips

The artistic branch growth on mature serviceberries makes them beautiful specimen plants or even shade trees in small gardens. The shrubbier forms can be grown along the edge of a woodland. In the wild, these trees are often found growing near water sources, where their fruit is relished by wildlife.

Recommended

Several species and hybrids are available. A few popular serviceberries are **A. arborea** (downy serviceberry, Juneberry), a small single- or multi-stemmed tree; **A. canadensis** (shadblow serviceberry), a large, upright, suckering shrub; and **A. x grandiflora** (apple serviceberry), a small, spreading, often multi-stemmed tree. All three share four-season interest.

A. canadensis (above), *A. arborea* (below)

Serviceberry fruit can be used in place of blueberries in any recipe, having a similar but generally sweeter flavor. In local rivers it is during the shad run that this plant blooms, hence it is sometimes called shadblow or shadbush "down Jersey."

Features: single- or multi-stemmed, deciduous large shrub or small tree; spring flowers; edible fruit; fall color; habit; bark
Height: 4–30' **Spread:** 4–30'
Hardiness: zones 3–9

Seven-Son Flower

Heptacodium

H. miconioides (above & below)

As a smallish tree with fragrant, white, September flowers followed by red sepals and fruit, seven-son flower makes a welcome addition to our plant palette.

Growing

Seven-son flower prefers **full sun** but tolerates partial shade. The soil should be of **average fertility, moist** and **well drained**, though this plant is fairly tolerant of most soil conditions, including dry and acidic soil.

Tips

This large shrub can be used in place of a shade tree on a small property. Planted near a patio or deck, the plant will provide light shade, and its fragrant flowers can be enjoyed in late summer. In a border it provides light shade to plants growing below it, and the dark green leaves make a good backdrop for bright perennial and annual flowers.

Seven-son flower's tolerance of dry and salty soils makes it useful where salty snow may be shoveled off walkways in winter and where watering will be minimal in summer.

Recommended

H. miconioides is a large, multi-stemmed shrub or small tree with peeling, tan bark and dark green leaves that may become tinged with purple in fall. Clusters of fragrant, creamy white flowers have persistent sepals (the outer ring of flower parts) that turn dark pink to bright red in mid- to late fall; these, along with the fruit capsules that change from green to rose-purple, are much more effective than the flowers.

Features: upright to spreading, multi-stemmed, deciduous shrub or small tree; habit; bark; fall flowers **Height:** 15–20' **Spread:** 8–15' **Hardiness:** zones 5–8

Smoke Bush

Cotinus

Bright fall color, adaptability, flowers of differing colors and variable sizes and forms make smoke bush and all its cultivars excellent additions to the garden.

Growing

Smoke bush grows well in **full sun** or **partial shade**. It prefers soil of **average fertility** that is **moist** and **well drained**, but it will adapt to all but very wet soils. It is an easy-to-grow plant.

Tips

Smoke bush can be used in a shrub or mixed border, as a single specimen or in groups. It is a good choice for a sandy area or rocky hillside planting. Shrubs grown for their colorful foliage can be cut back to the ground each spring—they will not flower, but foliage color will be intensified.

Recommended

C. obovatus (American smoke bush, chittamwood) is a New Jersey native that grows 20–30' tall. It is an upright tree with blue-green leaves that turn spectacular shades of yellow, orange, red and violet in fall.

C. coggygria is a bushy, rounded shrub that develops large, puffy plumes of flowers that start out green and gradually turn a pinky grey. The green foliage turns red, orange and yellow in fall. Many cultivars are available, including purple- or reddish purple-leaved selections.

C. coggygria 'Royal Purple' (above), *C. coggygria* (below)

Try encouraging a clematis vine to wind its way through the spreading branches of a smoke bush.

Also called: smoke tree **Features:** bushy, rounded, spreading, deciduous tree or shrub; early-summer flowers; summer and fall foliage **Height:** 10–30' **Spread:** 10–15' **Hardiness:** zones 4–8

Snowbell

Styrax

S. *obassia* (both photos)

Snowbells are easy to admire for their delicate, shapely appearance and dangling flowers clustered along the undersides of the branches.

Growing

Snowbells grow well in **full sun, partial shade** or **light shade**. The soil should be **fertile, humus rich, neutral to acidic, moist** and **well drained**.

Plant a snowbell next to your patio so you can admire the flowers from below as you stretch out in a lounge chair.

Tips

Snowbells can be used to provide light shade in shrub or mixed borders. They can also be included in woodland gardens, and they make fragrant specimens near entryways or patios.

Recommended

S. obassia (fragrant snowbell) is a broad, columnar tree that bears white flowers in long clusters at the branch ends in early summer.

Another commonly available species, *S. japonica* (Japanese snowbell) is not recommended because it is becoming invasive in native forests.

Features: upright, rounded, spreading or columnar, deciduous tree; late-spring to early-summer flowers; foliage; habit **Height:** 20–40' **Spread:** 20–30' **Hardiness:** zones 4–8

Sourwood
Oxydendrum

O. arboreum (both photos)

Native to the east coast, sourwood is underused as an ornamental tree. It has mid-summer flowers followed by brilliant fall color in shades of bright red with flat sprays of small green fruit that create a colorful contrast.

Growing
Sourwood grows well in **light shade** or **partial shade** in a sheltered location. The soil should be **fertile, acidic, moist** and **well drained**.

Tips
Native to open woodlands and streamsides, these small trees make an excellent addition to a lightly shaded garden. They can be included in woodland gardens and shaded borders.

Recommended
O. arboreum is a large shrub or small tree native to eastern North America. It is conical or columnar in habit and has glossy, green leaves that turn bright yellow, red and purple in fall. It bears large clusters of small, white flowers in late summer and fall.

This tree has several herbal uses. A tea made from the leaves is widely used by mountain climbers as a thirst-quencher. The pioneers used the sap as one ingredient in a tonic to lower fevers, and the bitter bark was chewed to soothe mouth pains. It is appreciated by beekeepers, as it makes for a sweet, delicate honey—surprising considering that all parts of the tree are bitter and sour.

Features: conical to columnar, deciduous large shrub or tree; summer and fall foliage; white flowers **Height:** 25–50'
Spread: 25–30' **Hardiness:** zones 5–9

Spruce
Picea

Spruce trees are often synonymous with Christmas trees in many areas and are one of the most commonly grown evergreens. Grow spruces where they have enough room to spread; then let them branch all the way to the ground.

Growing
Spruce trees grow best in **full sun**. The soil should be **deep, moist, well drained** and **neutral to acidic**. These trees generally don't like hot, dry or polluted conditions. Spruces are best grown from small, young stock, as they dislike being transplanted when larger or more mature.

Tips
Spruces are used as specimen trees. The dwarf and slow-growing cultivars can also be used in shrub or mixed borders.

Recommended
Spruce is a generally upright, pyramidal tree, but cultivars may be low growing, wide spreading or even weeping in habit. **P. abies** (Norway spruce), **P. glauca** (white spruce), **P. omorika** (Serbian spruce), **P. pungens** (Colorado spruce) and their cultivars are popular and commonly available.

P. glauca 'Conica' (above)
P. pungens var. glauca 'Moerheim' (below)

Oil-based pesticides such as dormant oil can take the blue out of your blue-needled spruces. Growth that fills in after this will have the blue color.

Features: conical or columnar, evergreen tree or shrub; foliage; cones; habit **Height:** 2–80' **Spread:** 2–25' **Hardiness:** zones 2–8

Stewartia

Stewartia

This lovely tree adds beauty to your garden all year, with dark green summer foliage, summer flowers, colorful fall foliage and exfoliating bark.

Growing

Stewartia grows well in **full sun** or **light shade**. The soil should be of **average to high fertility, humus rich, neutral to acidic, moist** and **well drained**. Provide shelter from strong winds. Transplant this tree when it is very young, as the roots resent being disturbed.

Tips

Stewartia is used as a specimen tree and in group plantings. It makes a good companion for rhododendron and azalea because stewartia will provide the light shade they enjoy, and all these plants grow well in similar soil conditions.

Recommended

S. pseudocamellia is a broad, columnar or pyramidal tree. White flowers with showy, yellow stamens appear in mid-summer. The dark green leaves turn shades of yellow, orange, scarlet and reddish purple in fall. The bark is scaly and exfoliating, leaving the trunk mottled with gray, orange, pink and reddish brown. Cultivars are available.

S. pseudocamellia (above)

Pretty, cinnamon-brown bark is exceptional and is the reason stewartia is a prominent specimen in the winter landscape. Don't be concerned if the bark doesn't put on a display when first planted. It takes several years for the tree to mature enough for the flaking to develop.

Also called: Japanese stewartia
Features: broad, conical or rounded, deciduous tree; mid-summer flowers; summer and fall foliage; exfoliating bark **Height:** 20–35'
Spread: 20–35' **Hardiness:** zones 5–7

Summersweet Clethra
Clethra

C. *alnifolia* 'Paniculata' (above & below)

This New Jersey native is one of the best shrubs for adding summer fragrance to your garden, and it attracts butterflies and other pollinators.

Growing
Summersweet clethra grows best in **light shade** or **partial shade**. The soil should be **fertile, humus rich, acidic, moist to wet** and **well drained**, but plants are adaptable to a wide range of conditions, including sunny sites, dry or alkaline soil and even winter salt spray. Keep in mind, though, that these swamp natives produce the most fragrant flowers when given adequate moisture.

Tips
Although not aggressive, this shrub tends to sucker, forming a colony of stems. Use it in a border or in a woodland garden. The light shade along the edge of a woodland is also an ideal location.

Recommended
C. alnifolia is a large, rounded, upright, colony-forming shrub. It grows 3–8' tall, spreading 3–6' and bearing attractive spikes of white flowers in mid- to late summer. The foliage turns yellow in fall. Several cultivars are available, including the pink-flowered RUBY SPICE and the compact **'Hummingbird.'**

Summersweet clethra is useful in damp, shaded gardens, where the late-season, fragrant flowers are much admired and appreciated by butterflies, hummingbirds and people.

Also called: sweet pepperbush, clethra
Features: rounded, suckering, deciduous shrub; fragrant, summer flowers; attractive habit; colorful fall foliage **Height:** 2–8'
Spread: 3–8' **Hardiness:** zones 3–9

Sweetspire
Itea

This popular summer bloomer has pendant clusters of fragrant flowers and stunning, vibrant red fall color.

Growing

Sweetspire grows well in all light conditions from **full sun to full shade**, though best fall foliage color develops in full sun. Habit is more open and arching in full sun and upright in shade. The soil should be **fertile** and **moist**, though plants adapt well to a range of conditions and are quite drought tolerant once established.

Tips

This shrub is excellent for low-lying and moist areas of the garden. It grows well near streams and water features. It is also great for plantings near decks, patios and pathways, where the fragrant flowers can be fully enjoyed.

Recommended

I. virginica is an upright to arching, suckering shrub. It usually grows 3–5' tall, but it can grow up to 10' tall, with an equal or greater spread. Spikes of fragrant, white flowers appear in late spring or early summer, and the leaves turn shades of purple and red in fall. **'Henry's Garnet'** bears many long, white flower spikes and consistently develops dark red-purple fall color.

I. virginica 'Henry's Garnet' (above), *I. virginica* (below)

Sweetspire is one of the most useful shrubs to include in damp, low-lying areas in the garden.

Features: upright to arching, deciduous shrub; fall color; fragrant, white, late-spring to early-summer flowers **Height:** 3–5'
Spread: 3–5' or more **Hardiness:** zones 5–9

Viburnum

Viburnum

V. opulus (above)
V. plicatum var. tomentosum (below)

Good fall color, attractive form, shade tolerance, scented flowers and attractive fruit put viburnums in a class by themselves.

Growing

Viburnums grow well in **full sun, partial shade** or **light shade**. The soil should be of average fertility, moist and well drained. Viburnums tolerate both alkaline and acidic soils.

The beautiful flowers are followed by fruit, which is more plentiful when more than one plant of a species is grown.

Tips

Viburnums can be used in borders and woodland gardens. Most do best in light shade, where their blooms are appreciated and their berries eaten by songbirds.

Recommended

Many viburnum species, hybrids and cultivars are available, including **V. carlesii** (Korean spice viburnum), a dense, bushy, rounded, deciduous shrub with white or pink, spicy-scented flowers (zones 5–8); **V. opulus** (European cranberrybush, Guelder-rose), a rounded, spreading, deciduous shrub with lacy-looking flower clusters (zones 3–8); **V. plicatum var. tomentosum** (doublefile viburnum), with a graceful, horizontal branching pattern that gives the shrub a layered effect and lacy-looking, white flower clusters (zones 5–8); and **V. trilobum** (American cranberrybush, high bush cranberry), a dense, rounded shrub with clusters of white flowers followed by edible, red fruit (zones 2–7).

Features: bushy or spreading, evergreen, semi-evergreen or deciduous shrub; flowers (some fragrant); summer and fall foliage; fruit; habit **Height:** 18"–20' **Spread:** 18"–15' **Hardiness:** zones 2–8

Witch-Hazel

Hamamelis

H. x intermedia 'Jelena' (above)
H. x intermedia (right)

Witch-hazel is an investment in happiness. Some bloom in late fall, others in winter and still others in spring. The flowers last for weeks, and their sweet, spring-like fragrance awakens the senses. Then in fall, the handsome leaves develop overlapping bands of orange, yellow and red.

Growing

Witch-hazels grow best in a sheltered spot with **full sun** or **light shade**. The soil should be of **average fertility, neutral to acidic, moist** and **well drained**.

Tips

Witch-hazels work well individually or in groups. They can be used as specimen plants, in shrub or mixed borders and in woodland gardens. As small trees, they are ideal for space-limited gardens.

The unique flowers have long, narrow, crinkled petals that give the plant a spidery appearance when in bloom. If the weather gets too cold, the petals will roll up, protecting the flowers and extending the flowering season.

Recommended

H. **x** *intermedia* is a vase-shaped, spreading shrub that bears fragrant clusters of yellow, orange or red flowers. The leaves turn attractive shades of orange, red and bronze in fall. Cultivars with flowers in shades of red, yellow or orange are available. **'Arnold's Promise'** is one of the most popular cultivars, with large, fragrant, bright yellow or yellow-orange flowers.

Features: spreading, deciduous shrub or small tree; fragrant, winter and early-spring flowers; summer and fall foliage; habit
Height: 6–20' **Spread:** 6–20'
Hardiness: zones 5–9

Apothecary's Rose

Species Rose

This fragrant rose has been cultivated since the 13th century and was used in herbal medicines to treat inflammation, aches and pains and insomnia.

Growing

Apothecary's Rose prefers **full sun** but tolerates afternoon shade. The soil should be **average to fertile, slightly acidic, humus rich, moist** and **well drained**. The suckers it produces should be removed once flowering is complete.

Tips

Apothecary's Rose can be grown as a specimen, in a shrub border or as a hedge. It can be naturalized or used to prevent soil erosion on a bank too steep for mowing. The flowers are very fragrant; plant this shrub near windows, doors and frequently used pathways.

Recommended

Rosa gallica '**Officinalis**' is a bushy, rounded, vigorous, disease-resistant shrub with bristly stems and dark green leaves. One flush of semi-double flowers is produced each year in late spring or early summer. *Rosa gallica* '**Versicolor**' has white or light pink flowers with darker pink splashes and stripes.

Dried petals from Apothecary's Rose were steeped in wine as a cure for hangovers from the time of the Romans through to the Middle Ages. It can be difficult to find except from antique rose sources, which are often mail order.

Also called: Red Damask, Red Rose of Lancaster **Features:** rounded habit; fresh and intensely fragrant, crimson purple to pink-ish red, early-summer flowers; dark red hips **Height:** 30"–4' **Spread:** 30"–4' **Hardiness:** zones 3–10

Blue Girl

Hybrid Tea Rose

*A*lthough not quite blue, the lovely mauve flowers are stunning and appear abundantly if the plant is fed and watered consistently.

Growing

Blue Girl grows best in **full sun** in a warm, sheltered location. The soil should be **fertile, humus rich, slightly acidic, moist** and **well drained**. Amend the soil with additional organic matter to improve its nutrient content, texture, water retention and drainage. Sprinkle soil and foliage with copper or sulfur for a natural way to combat black spot. Contact your local rose society for other natural recipes and environmentally safe chemical alternatives to use on roses.

Tips

Blue Girl, with its lovely flowers, is best used as a specimen plant, but it can be used in a mixed border with shallow-rooted plants that will not compete too much for water and nutrients.

Recommended

Rosa **'Blue Girl'** is a vigorous, shrubby rose with semi-glossy, dark green leaves. It produces fruity-scented, double flowers from spring to fall. Although it is susceptible to black spot, this rose is vigorous enough to grow past any infections.

These roses thrive when given a good soil and when grown where their foliage won't get frequently wetted by overhead sprinklers.

Features: shrubby habit; pink buds open to mauve, spring to fall flowers **Height:** 2–4'
Spread: 24–36" **Hardiness:** zones 6–10

Cary Grant

Hybrid Tea Rose

This beautiful rose has long-stemmed blooms in a brilliant shade of red or orange with a wonderful fragrance that permeates the air. It's sure to create a striking focal point in your garden.

This is a tremendously easy and rewarding rose to grow. It was commissioned by Cary Grant's wife, Barbara, for her husband as a Valentine's Day gift in 1986.

Growing

Cary Grant grows best in **full sun** in a warm, sheltered location. The soil should be **fertile, humus rich, slightly acidic, moist** and **well drained**. Amend the soil with compost or other organic matter to improve its nutrient content, texture, water retention and drainage.

Tips

Cary Grant makes an excellent specimen plant and blends well into a mixed border. It can even be used to create an attractive informal hedge.

Recommended

Rosa **'Cary Grant'** is a sturdy plant with glossy, dark green leaves. It produces huge, fully double, very fragrant flowers from spring to fall. It is disease resistant.

Features: shrubby habit; huge, fragrant, orange to scarlet, spring to fall flowers
Height: 2–4' **Spread:** 2–4'
Hardiness: zones 5–9

Eden

Climbing Romantica Rose

This bushy, vigorous climber has delightful large, fragrant, old-fashioned blooms in soft shades of pink, cream and yellow. These, combined with its sturdy growth and deep green foliage, make it perfect to grow on lamp posts and gazebos.

Growing

Eden grows best in **full sun**. The soil should be **average to fertile, humus rich, slightly acidic, moist** and **well drained**. This rose is disease resistant.

Tips

Train Eden to grow up pergolas, walls, pillars, arbors, trellises and fences. With some judicious pruning, this rose can be trained to form a bushy shrub or hedge.

Recommended

Rosa **'Eden'** is a vigorous climber with upright, arching canes and semi-glossy, light green foliage. It bears large, double, pink-tinged, creamy white to yellow flowers in a main flush in early summer and sporadically until fall.

White Eden is another nice climbing rose. Plentiful large, old fashioned, fragrant, white flowers almost 5" across mix well with red and pink roses. Its disease resistance makes it valuable for all landscapes.

Features: semi-glossy, light green foliage; climbing habit; fragrant, creamy white and yellow, pink-tinged flowers **Height:** 8–10' **Spread:** 8–10' **Hardiness:** zones 5–10

Hansa
Rugosa Shrub Rose

Hansa, first introduced in 1905, is one of the most durable, long-lived and versatile roses.

Growing
Hansa grows best in **full sun**. The soil should be **average to fertile, humus rich, slightly acidic, moist** and **well drained**, but this durable rose adapts to most soils, from sandy to silty clay. Remove a few of the oldest canes every few years to keep plants blooming vigorously.

Rosa rugosa is a wide-spreading plant with disease-resistant foliage, a trait it has passed on to many hybrids and cultivars. Its fragrant petals are good for jams, potpourri and rose water, and its hips, rich in vitamin C, can be used for teas.

Tips
Rugosa roses like Hansa make good additions to mixed borders and beds, and can also be used as hedges or as specimens. They are often used on steep banks to prevent soil erosion. Their prickly branches deter people from walking across flower beds and compacting the soil.

Recommended
Rosa 'Hansa' is a bushy shrub with arching canes and leathery, deeply veined, bright green leaves. The double flowers are produced all summer. The bright orange hips persist into winter. Other Rugosa roses include '**Blanc Double de Coubert**,' which produces white, double flowers all summer.

Features: dense, arching habit; clove-scented, mauve purple or mauve red, early-summer to fall flowers; orange-red hips
Height: 4–5' **Spread:** 5–6'
Hardiness: zones 3–9

Knockout

Modern Shrub Rose

This series of roses includes some of the best new shrub roses to hit the market in years. They are now available in more colors than ever on nearly indestructible plants.

Growing

Knockout grows best in **full sun**. The soil should be **fertile, humus rich, slightly acidic, moist** and **well drained**. This rose blooms most prolifically in warm weather but has deeper red flowers in cooler weather. Deadhead lightly to keep the plant tidy and to encourage prolific blooming.

Tips

This vigorous, attractive rose makes a good addition to a mixed bed or border, and it looks good when planted in groups of three or more. It can be mass planted to create a large display or grown singly as an equally attractive specimen.

Recommended

Rosa 'Knockout' has an attractive, rounded form with glossy, green leaves that turn to shades of burgundy in fall. The bright cherry red flowers are borne in clusters of 3–15 almost all summer and into fall. Orange-red hips last well into winter. You can also get **'Double Knockout,'** **'Pink Knockout'** and a light pink selection called **'Blushing Knockout.'** All have excellent disease resistance.

In New Jersey, this one often blooms from May until late November. If you've been afraid that roses need too much care, you'll appreciate the hardiness and disease-resistance of this low-maintenance beauty.

Also called: Knock Out **Features:** rounded habit; light tea rose-scented, early-summer to fall, cherry red flowers; disease resistant
Height: 3–4' **Spread:** 3–4'
Hardiness: zones 4–10

Pat Austin

English (Austin) Shrub Rose

David Austin roses are famous for their scent, and Pat Austin is no exception. The fragrance of these roses is fruity and sharp. Like all roses, they should be picked and enjoyed in a vase on your table or nightstand.

Growing

Pat Austin grows best in **full sun** in a warm, sheltered location. The soil should be **fertile, humus rich, slightly acidic, moist** and **well drained**. Deadhead to keep plants tidy and to encourage continuous blooming.

Tips

Austin roses such as Pat Austin have many uses and are often included in borders, as specimens and in containers. Plant Pat Austin near a window, door or pathway where its fragrance can best be enjoyed.

Recommended

Rosa **'Pat Austin'** forms a rounded shrub with dark green, glossy foliage and flexible canes that sway or bend under the weight of the double flowers. Pat Austin is one of many Austin roses that are also available in shades of pink, orange, apricot, yellow and white.

Pat Austin was introduced in 2002 by David Austin Roses Ltd. and is named in honor of David Austin's wife.

Features: attractive, rounded habit; fruity-scented, coppery amber or yellow, early-summer to fall flowers **Height:** 3–4' **Spread:** 3–4' **Hardiness:** zones 5–9

Red Eden

Climbing Rose

This is a new, deep burgundy red rose that will delight those who like bold colors. The lush flowers on this vigorous climber are plentiful from spring through fall. Another plus for this awesome plant is its disease resistance.

Growing

Red Eden grows best in **full sun**. The soil should be **average to fertile, humus rich, slightly acidic, moist** and **well drained**.

Tips

Train Red Eden to grow up pergolas, walls, pillars, arbors, trellises and fences. With some judicious pruning, this rose can be trained to form a bushy shrub or hedge.

Recommended

Rosa **'Red Eden'** is a vigorous climber with upright, arching canes and semiglossy, dark green foliage tinged with red. It bears large, fully double, crimson red flowers plentifully from early summer until fall.

Climbing roses sometimes take a few years to develop a lush, romantic look. Many rose societies give recipes that use household products to enrich the soil and increase rose vigor.

Features: semi-glossy, red-tinged, dark green foliage; climbing habit; lightly fragrant, crimson red flowers **Height:** 10–12' **Spread:** 5–8' **Hardiness:** zones 5–9

Rosa glauca

Species Rose

This species rose is a gardener's dream; it is hardy and disease resistant and has striking foliage in summer and colorful hips in winter.

Growing

Rosa glauca grows best and develops the most contrasting foliage color in **full sun**; in partial shade or full shade, the blooms and hips will be sparse, but the foliage will still be handsome. The soil should be **average to fertile, humus rich, slightly acidic, moist** and **well drained**, but this rose adapts to most New Jersey soil, from sand to silty clay.

Remove a few of the oldest canes to the ground every few years to encourage younger, more colorful stems to grow in. Removing spent flowers won't prolong the blooming period, and the more flowers you leave, the more hips will form.

Tips

With its unusual blue-toned leaves, pink blooms and bright hips, this plant is a year round charmer. It makes a good addition to mixed borders and beds, and it can also be used as a hedge or specimen.

Recommended

Rosa glauca (*R. rubrifolia*) is a bushy shrub with arching, purple-tinged canes and delicate, purple-tinged, blue-green leaves. The single, star-shaped flowers bloom in clusters in late spring. The dark red hips persist until spring.

Also called: Red-leaved Rose
Features: dense, arching habit; purple- or red-tinged foliage; mauve pink, white-centered, late-spring flowers; persistent, dark red hips
Height: 6–10' **Spread:** 5–6'
Hardiness: zones 2–9

Rouge Royale

Shrub Romantica Rose

Rouge Royale's lush, romantic flowers have at least 80 petals and a strong, fruity, citrus fragrance. They are long-lasting, both on the plant and in a vase.

Growing

Rouge Royale grows best in **full sun** in a warm, sheltered location. The soil should be **fertile, humus rich, slightly acidic, moist** and **well drained**. Amend the soil with compost or other organic matter to improve its nutrient content, texture, water retention and drainage.

Tips

Rouge Royale makes an excellent specimen plant and blends well into a mixed border. It can even be used to create an attractive informal hedge.

Recommended

Rosa 'Rouge Royale' is a sturdy plant with glossy, green leaves. It produces fully double, berry- and citrus-scented flowers from spring to fall. The flowers are raspberry red, opening from dark red buds. It is disease and heat resistant.

Like many other beautiful roses, this one can be preserved or dried in silica gel. The preserved flowers keep their fresh appearance and can be used on wreaths, in arrangements or to top a bowl of rose petal potpourri.

Features: shrubby habit; fragrant, orange to scarlet, spring to fall flowers **Height:** 3–4' **Spread:** 3–4' **Hardiness:** zones 5–9

Sunblaze

Miniature Rose

Tips

Miniature roses like Sunblaze are useful as annual or perennial shrubs. They can be included in window boxes, planters and mixed containers. In a bed or border they can be grouped together or planted individually to accentuate specific areas. They can also be used as groundcovers or to create low hedges.

Recommended

Rosa 'Sunblaze' is a compact, bushy shrub with glossy, light to dark green foliage. It produces double flowers all summer. Cultivars include '**Golden Sunblaze**,' with yellow flowers; '**Mandarin Sunblaze**,' with orange flowers; '**Autumn Sunblaze**,' with scarlet flowers; '**Bridal Sunblaze**,' with white flowers; '**Candy Sunblaze**,' with hot pink flowers; '**Lavender Sunblaze**,' with lavender flowers; '**Gypsy Sunblaze**,' with scarlet and white flowers; and '**Raspberry Sunblaze**,' with raspberry red flowers.

These compact little plants look almost like azaleas from a distance, but unlike azaleas, Sunblaze roses bloom on and on throughout the season.

Growing

Sunblaze roses grow best in **full sun**. The soil should be **fertile, humus rich, slightly acidic, moist** and **well drained**. Deadhead and feed well to keep plants neat and to encourage continuous blooming.

The prolific buds and semi-open blooms can be collected and dried for crafts, necklaces and potpourri. The blooms are edible and are absolutely wonderful to use for decorating cakes.

Features: bushy habit; double, slightly fragrant, red, crimson, scarlet, orange, yellow, pink, lavender or white, early-summer to fall flowers **Height:** 12–18" **Spread:** 12–18" **Hardiness:** zones 5–10

Black-Eyed Susan Vine

Thunbergia

The simple flowers of black-eyed Susan vine give it a cheerful, welcoming appearance.

Growing

Black-eyed Susan vine does well in **full sun, partial shade** or **light shade**. Grow it in **fertile, moist, well-drained** soil that is **rich in organic matter**. Water well and fertilize with a time-release fertilizer for a strong vine and continuous flowering. This plant does not like a lot of heat, so keep it away from areas with reflected heat from a driveway or the siding of a house. Do not allow this vine to dry out, especially during a hot drought period.

Tips

Black-eyed Susan vines can be trained to twine up and around fences, walls, trees and shrubs. They are also attractive trailing down from the top of a rock garden or rock wall or growing in mixed containers and hanging baskets.

Recommended

T. alata is a vigorous, twining climber. It bears yellow flowers, often with dark centers, in summer and fall. Cultivars with large flowers in yellow, orange or white are available.

T. alata (above & below)

Remember that you will have to replant this tender plant each year. Cuttings taken in late summer can be grown indoors in winter.

Features: twining habit; yellow, orange or creamy white, dark-centered flowers
Height: 5' or more **Spread:** 5' or more
Hardiness: tender perennial treated as an annual

Carolina Jessamine
Gelsemium

G. sempervirens (above & below)

Notice the name is jessamine, not jasmine. This beautiful, fragrant plant is an energetic grower with bright yellow flowers in winter and early spring.

Growing

Carolina jessamine grows well in **full sun** or **partial shade** in a sheltered location. The soil should be of **average fertility, moist** and **well drained**. Cold and drying winds can damage this plant, particularly in winter when it is dormant and unable to replenish lost moisture.

Tips

This vigorous but not invasive vine blooms when little else does. It is a lovely plant to grow up the railings of a porch where the fragrant flowers can be enjoyed up close. It can also be grown up a strong trellis on a wall, up a fence, over an arbor or arch and up a pergola.

Recommended

G. sempervirens is a vigorous, twining evergreen vine that grows 10–20' tall. Clusters of fragrant, pale to bright yellow, funnel-shaped flowers are produced in spring and summer.

Plant annual, summer- and fall-flowering vines next to it each year to have color and bloom the entire growing season.

Features: twining habit; glossy foliage; fragrant, yellow, spring and summer flowers
Height: 10–20' **Spread:** 5–20'
Hardiness: zones 7–9

Clematis
Clematis

There are enough clematis plants with different flowering times that it is possible to have one in bloom all season.

Growing
Clematis plants prefer **full sun** but tolerate partial shade. The soil should be **fertile, humus rich, moist** and **well drained**. These vines enjoy warm, sunny weather, but the roots prefer to be cool. A thick layer of mulch or a planting of low, shade-providing perennials will protect the tender roots.

Many areas in New Jersey have very sandy soil, so gardeners need to be prepared to add a lot of compost to the soil for clematis plants. They are quite cold hardy but will fare best when protected from winter wind. The root ball of vining clematis should be planted about 2" beneath the surface of the soil.

Tips
Clematis vines can climb up structures such as trellises, railings, fences and arbors. They can also be allowed to grow over shrubs and up trees and can be used as groundcovers.

Recommended
There are many species, hybrids and cultivars of clematis. The flower form, blooming time and size of the plants can vary. Check with your local garden center to see what is available.

C. x jackmanii 'Rubra' (above), *C. x jackmanii* (below)

Be careful when weeding or cleaning up around base of these plants, as the slender stems are often accidentally snapped off at ground level.

Features: twining habit; blue, purple, pink, yellow, red or white, early- to late-summer flowers; decorative seed-heads
Height: 10–17' or more **Spread:** 5' or more
Hardiness: zones 3–8

Climbing Hydrangea
Hydrangea

H. anomala subsp. *petiolaris* (above & below)

A mature climbing hydrangea can cover an entire wall, and with its dark, glossy leaves and delicate, lacy flowers, it is quite possibly one of the most stunning climbing plants available.

Growing

Hydrangeas prefer **partial shade** or **light shade** but tolerate both full sun and full shade. The soil should be of **average to rich fertility, humus rich, moist** and **well drained**. These plants perform best in cool, moist conditions, so be sure to add a layer of mulch, especially in sunny locations.

Tips

Climbing hydrangea climbs up trees, walls, fences, pergolas and arbors. It clings to walls by means of aerial roots, so it needs no support, just a somewhat textured surface. It also grows over rocks, can be used as a groundcover and can be trained to form a small tree or shrub.

Recommended

H. anomala subsp. *petiolaris* (*H. petiolaris*) is a clinging vine with glossy, dark green leaves that sometimes turn an attractive yellow in fall. For more than a month in mid-summer, the vine is covered with white, lacy-looking flowers, and the entire plant appears to be veiled in a lacy mist.

Climbing hydrangea will produce the most flowers when it is exposed to some direct sunlight each day.

Features: flowers; clinging habit; exfoliating bark **Height:** 50–80' **Spread:** 50–80'
Hardiness: zones 4–9

Hardy Jasmine

Jasminum

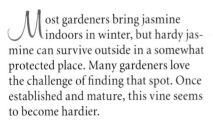

Most gardeners bring jasmine indoors in winter, but hardy jasmine can survive outside in a somewhat protected place. Many gardeners love the challenge of finding that spot. Once established and mature, this vine seems to become hardier.

Growing

Hardy jasmine grows well in **full sun** or **partial shade**. The soil should be **fertile** and **well drained**. Thin out after flowering when growth becomes overcrowded. If this plant is grown in a container or hanging basket, you may find it best to move it to a sheltered location in winter, as plants are not as hardy in containers as when grown in the ground.

Tips

Hardy jasmines are a welcome addition to large mixed containers; they can be grown up a decorative support or allowed to trail over the edges. They also make an interesting choice in hanging baskets, where they trail over the edges and climb up the hangers. In the garden they will grow up trellises, arbors, pergolas and even shrubs.

Recommended

J. officinale is a vigorous, twining, deciduous or semi-evergreen climber. It bears clusters of fragrant, white flowers and is a good choice to grow near an entryway so that its heavenly scent can be enjoyed from late spring to fall. It is hardy to zone 6 or 7 in a sheltered spot near the warm foundation of a house.

J. x stephanense (above)

J. x stephanense is a vigorous, twining, deciduous vine with green, sometimes cream-flushed foliage. It bears loose clusters of mildly fragrant, pale pink flowers in flushes from late spring to mid-summer. In a sheltered location, vines may survive the winter in zone 6.

For those who love tropical plants and like to give them a chance, hardy jasmine is a worthwhile challenge.

Features: twining habit; fragrant, pale pink, summer flowers **Height:** 10–15'
Spread: 5–15' **Hardiness:** 7–10; may survive in zone 6

Honeysuckle
Lonicera

Some honeysuckles can be rampant growers, but with careful consideration and placement, they won't overrun your garden. The fragrance of the flowers makes any effort worthwhile.

Growing
Honeysuckles grow well in **full sun** or **partial shade**. The soil should be **average to fertile, humus rich, moist** and **well drained**.

Tips
Honeysuckle can be trained to grow up a trellis, fence, arbor or other structure. In a large container near a porch, it will ramble over the edge of the pot and up the railings with reckless abandon.

Recommended
There are dozens of honeysuckle species, hybrids and cultivars. Check with your local garden center to see what is available. The following are two popular species.
L. caprifolium (Italian honeysuckle, Italian woodbine) bears fragrant, creamy white or yellow flowers in late spring and early summer.
L. sempervirens (trumpet honeysuckle, coral honeysuckle) bears orange or red flowers in late spring and early summer. Many cultivars and hybrids are available with flowers in yellow, red or scarlet, including *L.* x *brownii* **'Dropmore Scarlet,'** one of the hardiest of the climbing honeysuckles, cold hardy to zone 4. It bears bright red flowers for most of summer.

L. sempervirens (above)
L. x brownii 'Dropmore Scarlet' (below)

Features: late-spring and early-summer flowers; twining habit; fruit **Height:** 6–20'
Spread: 6–20' **Hardiness:** zones 5–8

Hops
Humulus

*I*f you sit near a hops vine for an afternoon, you might actually be able to watch it grow. I have noted 24" of growth in a single day in early summer.

Growing

Hops grow best in **full sun**. The soil should be **average to fertile, humus rich, moist** and **well drained**, but established plants adapt to most conditions, including drought if they are well watered for the first few years.

Tips

Hops quickly twine around any sturdy support to create a screen or to shade a patio or deck. Provide a pergola, arbor, porch rail or even a telephone pole for hops to grow up. Most trellises are too delicate for this vigorous vine.

Recommended

H. lupulus is a fast-growing, twining vine with rough-textured, bright green leaves and stems. The fragrant, cone-like flowers—produced on only the female plants and used to flavor and preserve beer—open pale green and ripen to beige. A cultivar with golden yellow foliage is available. Most of the available cultivars have been developed to add their unique flavors to the many types of beer.

H. lupulus (above & below)

As true perennials, hops send up new shoots from ground level each year. The previous year's growth needs to be cleared away each fall or spring. The blooms are lovely and can be dried and used in herb wreaths, arrangements and sleep or dream pillows.

Features: twining habit; dense growth; cone-like, pale green, late-summer flowers that ripen to beige **Height:** 10–20' **Spread:** 10–20' **Hardiness:** zones 3–8

Hyacinth Bean
Lablab

L. purpureus (above & below)

The raw beans contain a cyanide-releasing chemical and should never be eaten. In their native Africa, they are cooked in several changes of water to leach away the poison before they are eaten.

Typically we use hyacinth bean to climb trellises and walls, but another intriguing application is to let it roam on the ground through the feet of other plants. It has beautiful blooms, pods and foliage. Perhaps it is the bean stalk Jack climbed in the fairy tale.

Growing
Hyacinth bean prefers **full sun**. The soil should be **fertile, moist** and **well drained**. This plant is a legume and will enrich your soil with nitrogen.

Tips
Plant hyacinth bean near a trellis, balcony or garden structure or against a fence. If you grow it as a groundcover, make sure it doesn't engulf smaller plants.

Recommended
L. purpureus (*Dolichos lablab*) is a vigorous, twining vine. It can grow up to 30' tall, but when grown as an annual it grows about 10–15' tall. It bears many purple or white flowers over summer, followed by deep purple pods.

Also called: Egyptian bean, lablab bean
Features: twining vine; purple or white flowers in summer; purple or purple-flushed seed pods in fall **Height:** 10–15' **Spread:** 5–15'
Hardiness: tender perennial treated as an annual; may survive in zone 7

Japanese Hydrangea Vine

Schizophragma

This vine is similar in appearance to climbing hydrangea, but it has a few interesting cultivars to add variety.

Growing

Japanese hydrangea vine grows well in **full sun** or **partial shade**. The soil should be **average to fertile, humus rich, moist** and **well drained**.

This vine will have trouble clinging to a smooth-surfaced wall. Attach a few supports to the wall and tie the vines to these. The dense growth will eventually hide the support.

Tips

This vine will cling to any rough surface and looks attractive climbing a wall, fence, tree, pergola or arbor. It can also be used as a groundcover on a bank or allowed to grow up or over a rock wall.

Recommended

S. hydrangeoides is an attractive, climbing vine similar in appearance to climbing hydrangea. It bears lacy clusters of white flowers in mid-summer. **'Moonlight'** has silvery blue foliage. **'Roseum'** bears clusters of pink flowers.

This elegant, yet easy to grow vine adds a touch of glamour to even the most ordinary-looking home.

S. hydrangeoides (above & below)

Features: clinging habit; dark green or silvery foliage; white or pink flowers **Height:** up to 40' **Spread:** up to 40' **Hardiness:** zones 5–8

Moon Flower

Ipomoea

I. alba (above & below)

*L*uminous white flowers are produced in abundance and open late in the day to be best enjoyed while relaxing in the failing light of evening.

Growing

Moon flower grows best in **full sun**. The soil should be of **poor to average fertility, light** and **well drained**, though these plants adapt to most soil conditions. These plants twine around narrow objects to climb and must be provided with a trellis or wires if grown against a fence with broad boards, a wall or any other surface they won't be able to wind around.

Tips

On trellises and fences or as groundcovers, moon flowers will grow over any objects they encounter. They can also be grown in large hanging baskets or containers, where they will spill over the edges.

Recommended

I. alba is a twining climber that bears sweet-scented, white flowers that open only at night.

As evening falls, the huge, white blossoms pour forth their sweet nectar, attracting night-flying moths.

Features: fast-growing; twining habit; flowers; foliage **Height:** 6–15' **Spread:** 6–15' **Hardiness:** tender perennial grown as an annual

Native Hydrangea Vine

Decumaria

This vine is an early-summer bloomer. Handsome, glossy, dark green foliage sets off lacy clusters of creamy white, honey-scented flowers.

Growing

Native hydrangea vine grows well in **full sun** or in a sheltered location with some shade in colder areas. The soil should be **fertile** and **moist**. A winter mulch will protect the roots from temperature fluctuations and drought.

Tips

In the wild, these vines are commonly found growing in forests up the trunks and branches of trees. As they cling using aerial roots, they can be grown up most textured walls as well as arbors, pergolas, fences or even a tree in your garden. Native hydrangea vine doesn't bloom if it is not climbing, but it can still be used as a ground-cover in damp areas.

Recommended

D. barbara is a woody climber that uses aerial roots to cling to the surface it's climbing. It has glossy, dark green foliage and bears clusters of white, fragrant flowers in summer.

D. barbara (above & below)

This plant is easy to grow in a shady garden where a vine is needed. It is not aggressive, and the delicate aerial rootlets will not hurt trees. It is a native flowering vine that attracts butterflies.

Features: deciduous climber; glossy, dark green foliage; white, summer flowers
Height: up to 30' **Spread:** 5–30'
Hardiness: zones 6–9

Passionflower
Passiflora

P. caerulea (above & below)

In Bermuda, passionflower is made into perfume. It is considered an herb by some and is used in some sleep-aid capsules found in health food stores.

Mesmerizing with exotic fragrance and beauty, passionflower is sure to attract attention in your garden.

Growing
Passionflower grows well in **full sun** or **partial shade** in a location sheltered from wind and cold. The soil should be of **average fertility, moist** and **well drained**.

Tips
Passionflower is a popular addition to mixed containers and creates an unusual focal point near a door or other entryway. Provided with a trellis or other structure, it will climb all summer, though not as much as some of the other annual vines. A few are hardy to zone 6, and these vines may survive winter in many New Jersey gardens.

Recommended
P. caerulea is a vigorous, woody climber with deeply lobed leaves. It bears unusual, purple-banded, purple-white flowers all summer. It can grow up to 30' tall but usually only grows 5–10' over the course of a summer.

P. incarnata is a lovely climber that clings to the climbing surface with tendrils. It bears pale purple or white flowers with purple and white coronas all summer. This native is cold hardy to zone 6. The vine dies back after frost, but the roots remain alive and send up foliage in spring around May.

Features: exotic, purple-white flowers; attractive foliage **Height:** 5–10' **Spread:** variable **Hardiness:** zones 6–9; often grown as an annual

Calla Lily

Zantedeschia

There are few plants that can rival the elegant simplicity of calla lily's flowers and foliage.

Growing

Calla lilies grow best in **full sun**. The soil should be **fertile, humus rich** and **moist to wet**. Callas grown in planters can be kept in a cool, bright room in winter and should be watered very little while dormant. Some, like the cultivar 'White Giant,' will come back year after year, especially in the southern half of New Jersey. They have more of a chance of making it through winter outside when situated in a protected spot and covered with a 6" layer of mulch.

Tips

Beautiful and exotic, calla lilies will give your garden a tropical appearance. Their moisture-loving nature makes them an ideal choice to include in a water feature, if you have one. They can be grown in large planters as specimens or mixed with other plants. They can also be included in borders if they are kept well watered.

Recommended

Z. aethiopica forms a large clump of arrow-shaped, glossy, green leaves. It bears white flowers from late spring to mid-summer. Cultivars are available. **'White Giant'** is hardy to zone 7a. (Zones 8–10)

Z. elliotiana (yellow calla, golden calla) is a tender perennial that forms a large

Z. aethiopica 'Little Gem' (above), Z. 'Flame' (below)

clump of white-spotted, dark green, heart-shaped leaves. It bears yellow flowers in summer. Cultivars are available.

Z. hybrids are tender perennials that have been developed from crosses between other species and have variable leaf shapes and colors and flowers in a wide range of colors.

Features: heart-, arrow- or sword-shaped, dark green, sometimes spotted leaves; spring or summer, white, yellow, pink, orange, red, purple or bicolored flowers **Height:** 24–36" **Spread:** 12–24" **Hardiness:** zones 8–10, or tender perennial grown as an annual

Crocus
Crocus

C. x vernus cultivar (above & below)

Crocuses are harbingers of spring. They often appear, as if by magic, in full bloom from beneath the melting snow.

Growing

Crocuses grow well in **full sun** or **light shade**. The soil should be of **poor to average fertility, gritty** and **well drained**. The corms are planted about 4" deep in fall.

Tips

Crocuses are almost always planted in groups. Drifts of crocuses can be planted in lawns to provide interest and color while the grass still lies dormant. They are nice to naturalize in gardens near doorways, mailboxes and driveways. Bulbs will soon multiply to form groups of plants that provide a bright welcome in spring.

Recommended

Many crocus species, hybrids and cultivars are available. The spring-flowering crocus most people are familiar with is **C. x vernus**, commonly called Dutch crocus. Many cultivars are available with flowers in shades of purple, yellow or white, sometimes bicolored or with darker veins.

Features: early-spring flowers **Height:** 2–6"
Spread: 2–4" **Hardiness:** zones 3–8

Daffodil

Narcissus

Many gardeners think of large, yellow, trumpet-shaped flowers when they think of daffodils, but there is plenty of variation in color, form and size amongst these cheerful spring bloomers.

Growing

Daffodils grow well in **full sun** or **light shade**. The soil should be **average to fertile, moist** and **well drained**. Bulbs should be planted in fall, 2–8" deep depending on the size of the bulb. The bigger the bulb, the deeper it should be planted. A rule of thumb is to measure the bulb from top to bottom and multiply that number by three to determine how deeply to plant.

Tips

Daffodils are often planted in the light shade beneath a tree or in a woodland garden where they can be left to naturalize. In mixed beds and borders, the summer foliage of other plants will hide the faded leaves. As much as you might be tempted to cut off spent foliage, just leave it or braid it until it dies naturally. The foliage feeds the bulb so that there will be blooms the next spring.

Recommended

Many species, hybrids and cultivars of daffodils are available. Flowers come in shades of white, yellow, peach, orange or pink and may also be bicolored. Blooms range from 1–6" across and can be solitary or borne in clusters. There are about 12 flower form categories.

Features: spring flowers **Height:** 4–24"
Spread: 4–12" **Hardiness:** zones 3–9

Fritillaria

Fritillaria

F. imperialis (above & below)

Fritillarias are sure to make for a real conversation piece, especially the ones with the unusual checkered blooms.

Growing

Fritillarias grow best in **full sun**. The soil should be **fertile** and very **well drained**. The bulbs are prone to rot, so plant them on their sides so that moisture doesn't collect in the hollow top. They should be planted four times their own height deep.

Tips

Certain fritillarias make a striking addition to a rock garden or well-drained mixed border. They can be grown in large pots and kept under an overhang or in an unheated garage or shed during winter to prevent the bulb from rotting.

Recommended

F. imperialis is an upright plant with narrow, bright green leaves. Flowers are produced in a pendant cluster that surrounds the stem and is topped by a cluster of leaves. It has a musky odor that is reputed to keep rodents out of the bulb garden. (Zones 5–9)

F. meleagris (checker lily, snake's head, leper lily, Guinea hen) has gray-green foliage and bears bell-shaped flowers in shades of reddish brown, purple, white or gray with a distinctive checkered pattern.

Features: orange, yellow, purple, white, gray, red or reddish brown, spring flowers
Height: 36" **Spread:** 6–12"
Hardiness: zones 3–9

Grecian Windflower

Anemone

A. blanda (above), A. blanda 'White Splendor' (below)

Hardy and easy to grow, Grecian windflower provides a lovely spring complement to brightly colored spring bloomers.

Growing

Grecian windflower grows best in **full sun**. The soil should be of **average fertility, light, sandy** and **well drained**.

Tips

Grecian windflower makes a beautiful addition to a border or rock garden. Small clumps dotted here and there will add to your spring display of color, celebrating the end of winter. This pretty, daisy-like bloomer is wonderful when naturalized in the garden.

Recommended

A. blanda is a low, spreading, tuberous species that bears blue, white or pink flowers in spring, followed by fluffy seed heads. **'Pink Star'** has pink flowers with yellow centers. **'White Splendor'** is a vigorous plant with white flowers.

Features: tuberous perennial; blue, pink or white, spring flowers; fluffy seed heads
Height: 6–8" **Spread:** 6–12"
Hardiness: zones 4–8

Hyacinth

Hyacinthus

H. orientalis cultivar (above & below)

In the mid-18th century, Madame de Pompadour, trendsetter and mistress of France's King Louis XV, ordered the gardens of Versailles filled with hyacinths and also had them forced to bloom inside the palace in winter.

Hyacinths originated in Turkey, and in the centuries since their introduction to the rest of the world, they have filled the spring air with sweet perfume.

Growing

Hyacinths grow best in **full sun** but tolerate partial shade. The soil should be of **average fertility, moist** and **well drained**. Plant bulbs 4–8" deep in fall. The colder your winters are, the deeper you should plant these bulbs.

Tips

Plant hyacinths in groups of three to seven amongst the other plants in your beds and borders for a bold splash of color and an unforgettable fragrance. After a few years, even the heftiest hybrids shed much of their thick coat of flowers and resemble more and more their humble ancestor. Thus naturalized, they develop a style that fits with many gardening tastes today.

Recommended

H. orientalis is a perennial bulb that forms a clump of strap-like leaves. A spike of fragrant, star-shaped flowers is produced in spring. The species bears light purple flowers, but many cultivars have been developed, and they come in a huge range of colors with much larger, showier flowers.

Features: spring flowers in shades of purple, blue, pink, red, yellow, orange or white
Height: 8–12" **Spread:** 3–6"
Hardiness: zones 5–9; often treated as an annual

Lily

Lilium

Decorative clusters of large, richly colored blooms grace these tall plants. Flowers are produced at differing times during the season, depending on the hybrid, and it is possible to have lilies blooming all season if a variety of cultivars are chosen.

Growing

Lilies grow best in **full sun** but like to have their roots shaded. The soil should be **rich in organic matter, fertile, moist** and **well drained**.

Tips

Lilies are often grouped in beds and borders and can be naturalized in woodland gardens and near water features. These plants are tall but narrow; plant at least three of them together to create some volume.

Recommended

The many species, hybrids and cultivars available are grouped by type. Visit your local garden center to see what is available. **Asiatic hybrids** bear clusters of flowers in early or mid-summer and are available in a wide range of colors. **Oriental hybrids** bear clusters of large, fragrant flowers in mid- and late summer. *L. superbum* (turk's cap lily) is a New Jersey native that bears large clusters of deep orange, dark-spotted flowers. The petals turn back, giving each bloom the appearance of a turban.

L. Asiatic hybrids (above), *L.* 'Stargazer' (below)

Lily bulbs should be planted in fall before the first frost, but can also be planted in spring if bulbs are available. Easter lilies purchased to enjoy indoors will bloom again in August and then the following June if they are planted out in spring.

Features: early-, mid- or late-season flowers in shades of orange, yellow, peach, pink, purple, red or white **Height:** 2–5' **Spread:** 12" **Hardiness:** zones 4–8

Snowdrops

Galanthus

G. nivalis (above & below)

Growing

Snowdrops prefer to grow in **partial shade** or **light shade** but tolerate all light conditions from full sun to full shade. The soil should be of **average fertility, humus rich, moist** and **well drained**. They prefer not to have their soil dry out completely in summer. Plant bulbs 4" deep and 2" apart. Divide or move plants as soon as possible after flowering is complete in spring.

Tips

Snowdrops are popular bulbs for naturalizing. They can be planted into mixed beds and borders, thriving at the feet of deciduous shrubs and in meadow plantings.

These are the first bulbs to bloom, often as early as January; their delicate, white, nodding flowers pierce through snow, giving us a taste of a still-distant spring.

Recommended

G. elwesii (giant snowdrop) forms a clump of bright green, strap-like leaves. It bears fragrant, white flowers in late winter and grows 5–12" tall.

G. nivalis (common snowdrop) forms a clump of long, narrow leaves. It bears small, white, fragrant flowers in winter and grows about 4" tall. **'Flore Pleno'** bears double flowers.

These lovely plants are adaptable and hardy, and most animals will not eat them.

Features: white, early-spring flowers
Height: 4–12" **Spread:** 2–6"
Hardiness: zones 3–9

Spanish Bluebells

Hyacinthoides

These bulbs form really good clumping masses as they mature, making Spanish bluebells one of the best for naturalizing. They can stick around for decades.

Growing

Spanish bluebells grow best in **light shade**. The soil should be of **average fertility, humus rich, moist** and **well drained**, though these bulbs are quite tolerant of a variety of soils. Plant bulbs about 3" deep in fall.

Tips

Include Spanish bluebells in woodland gardens and under shrubs in beds and borders, especially where early-blooming bulbs finish first. They fill in to provide long-lasting color.

Recommended

H. hispanica forms a clump of strap-like leaves and produces spikes of blue, bell-shaped flowers. It grows about 16" tall and spreads about 12". Cultivars with purple, white or pinkish purple flowers are also available.

H. hispanica cultivar (above), *H. hispanica* (below)

These blooms are pretty and long lasting as cut flowers. Native to Spain, Portugal and northern Africa, Spanish bluebells have been successfully grown in many parts of the world.

Also called: bluebell **Features:** blue, purple, white or pink, spring flowers; clump-forming habit; suitable for naturalizing **Height:** 12–18" **Spread:** 8–16" **Hardiness:** zones 4–9

Tulip
Tulipa

T. hybrids (above & below)

Tulips, with their beautiful, often garishly colored flowers, are a welcome sight as we enjoy the warm days of spring.

Growing

Tulips grow best in **full sun**. The flowers tend to bend toward the light in light shade or partial shade. The soil should be **fertile** and **well drained**. Plant bulbs in fall, 4–6" deep depending on the size of the bulb. Bulbs that have been cold treated can be planted in spring. Although tulips can repeat bloom, many hybrids perform best if planted new each year. Species and older cultivars are the best choices for naturalizing.

Tips

Tulips provide a great display when mass planted or planted in groups in flowerbeds and borders. They can also be grown in containers and can be forced to bloom early in pots indoors. Some of the species and older cultivars can be naturalized in meadow and wildflower gardens. These are the bulbs most often eaten by rodents.

Recommended

There are about 100 species of tulips and thousands of hybrids and cultivars. They are generally divided into 15 groups based on bloom time and flower appearance. They come in dozens of shades, with many bicolored or multi-colored varieties. Blue is the only shade not available. Check with your local garden center in early fall for the best selection.

Features: spring flowers in shades of red, scarlet, pink, purple, yellow, orange, cream or white, as well as bicolors and multi-colors
Height: 6–30" **Spread:** 2–8"
Hardiness: zones 3–8; often treated as annuals

Angelica

Angelica

This versatile herb has a variety of culinary uses. The leaves can be added to salads or stewed with rhubarb, the seeds can be used to flavor candies and baked goods and the stems can be candied and used to decorate cakes.

Growing

Angelica grows best in **full shade** or **partial shade**. The soil should be **fertile, loamy** and **moist**. These plants die after they have flowered; allow them to self-seed freely so that you're sure to have angelica reappear in your garden year after year.

Tips

These tall, eye-catching beauties are some of the more impressive specimens for the back of a shaded border. Their bold leaves and striking flower heads can brighten up a spot that might otherwise seem dull and dark.

Recommended

A. archangelica forms a dense, mounded clump of basal foliage the first year and stout stems bearing large, rounded clusters of greenish yellow flowers the second year.

A. archangelica (above & below)

Angelica is often treated as a biennial plant. It is actually a monocarpic perennial, which means it will come back each year until it flowers.

Features: fragrant stems, leaves and seeds; large, rounded flower clusters and seed heads
Height: 4–6' **Spread:** 3–4'
Hardiness: zones 3–9

Basil
Ocimum

The sweet, fragrant leaves of fresh basil add a delicious spicy, licorice-like flavor to salads and tomato-based dishes. Combined and simmered with a good olive oil, lots of garlic and plum tomatoes, it makes the best sauce in the world for angel hair pasta.

Growing

Basil grows best in a warm, sheltered location in **full sun**. The soil should be **fertile, moist** and **well drained**. Pinch tips regularly to encourage bushy growth. Plant out or direct sow seed after the danger of frost has passed in spring.

Tips

Although basil will grow best in a warm spot outdoors in the garden, it can be grown successfully in a pot by a bright sunny window indoors to provide you with fresh leaves all year.

O. basilicum 'Genovese' and 'Cinnamon' (above)
O. basilicum 'Genovese' (below)

Recommended

O. basilicum is one of the most popular culinary herbs. There are dozens of varieties, including ones with large or tiny, green or purple and smooth or ruffled leaves. Different strains of basil also have different flavors including lemon, cinnamon, anise and lime, as well as the distinctive Thai basil.

Features: fragrant, decorative leaves
Height: 12–24" **Spread:** 12–18"
Hardiness: tender annual

Chives
Allium

The delicate onion flavor of chives is best enjoyed fresh. Mix chives into dips or sprinkle them on salads and baked potatoes. The blooms are striking in the garden and in salads or herbal vinegars.

Growing

Chives grow best in **full sun**. The soil should be **fertile, moist** and **well drained**, but chives adapt to most soil conditions. These plants are easy to start from seed, but they do like the soil temperature to stay above 65° F before they will germinate, so seeds started directly in the garden are unlikely to sprout before early summer.

Tips

Chives are decorative enough to be included in a mixed or herbaceous border and can be left to naturalize. In an herb garden, chives should be given plenty of space to allow for self-seeding.

Recommended

A. schoenoprasum forms a clump of bright green, cylindrical leaves. Clusters of pinky purple flowers are produced in early and mid-summer. Varieties with white or pink flowers are available.

Be cautious when growing **A. tuberosum** (garlic chives). Beautiful and useful as they are with their white flowers blooming late in summer, if you let them go to seed, they will likely be everywhere in your garden, as they are far more aggressive self-seeders than ordinary chives.

A. schoenoprasum (above & below)

Chives are said to increase appetite and encourage good digestion.

Features: foliage; form; flowers
Height: 8–24" **Spread:** 12" or more
Hardiness: zones 3–9

Coriander • Cilantro

Coriandrum

Coriander is a multi-purpose herb. The leaves, called cilantro, are used in salads, salsas and soups. The seeds, called coriander, are used in cakes, pies, chutneys and marmalades. The flavor of each is quite distinct.

Growing

Coriander prefers **full sun** but benefits from partial shade during mid-summer heat. The soil should be **fertile, light** and **well drained**. These plants dislike humid conditions and do best during a dry summer. Sow successively every few weeks in spring and early summer for constant harvesting.

Tips

Coriander has pungent leaves and is best planted where people will not have to brush past it. It is, however, a delight to behold when in flower. Add a plant or two here and there throughout your borders and vegetable garden, both for the visual appeal and to attract beneficial insects.

C. sativum (above & below)

Recommended

C. sativum forms a clump of lacy basal foliage above which large, loose clusters of tiny, white flowers are produced. The seeds ripen in late summer and fall.

Features: form; foliage; flowers; seeds
Height: 18–24" **Spread:** 8–18"
Hardiness: annual

Dill

Anethum

Dill is majestic and beautiful in any garden setting. Its leaves and seeds are probably best known for their use as pickling herbs, though they have a wide variety of other culinary uses.

Growing

Dill grows best in **full sun** in a sheltered location out of strong winds. The soil should be of **poor to average fertility, moist** and **well drained**. Sow seeds every couple of weeks in spring and early summer to ensure a regular supply of leaves. Dill should not be grown near fennel because they will cross-pollinate, and the seeds of both plants will lose their distinct flavors.

Tips

With its feathery leaves, dill is an attractive addition to a mixed bed or border. It can be included in a vegetable garden but does well in any sunny location. It also attracts butterflies and predatory insects to the garden.

A. graveolens (above & below)

Recommended

A. graveolens forms a clump of feathery foliage. Clusters of yellow flowers are borne at the tops of sturdy stems.

Marinating a fillet of salmon with the leaves and seeds of dill makes a popular Scandinavian dish called gravalax.

Features: feathery, edible foliage; yellow, summer flowers; edible seeds **Height:** 2–5'
Spread: 12" or more **Hardiness:** annual

French Tarragon
Artemisia

The distinctive licorice-like flavor of tarragon lends itself to a wide variety of meat and vegetable dishes and is the key flavoring ingredient in Béarnaise sauce.

Growing

French tarragon grows best in **full sun** with good air circulation. The soil should be **average to fertile** and **well drained**. Pinch plants back early in the season to encourage bushy growth that is less prone to flopping over later in summer. Divide the plants every few years to keep them growing vigorously and to encourage the best-flavored leaves.

Tips

French tarragon can be included in borders as well as herb gardens and will grow quite well in containers.

Recommended

A. dracunculus var. *sativa* forms a clump of upright, leafy stems. The leaves are narrow, dark green and very fragrant.

A. dracunculus var. sativa (above & below)

French tarragon is the preferred culinary selection. Russian tarragon is weedy and has no culinary value. Mexican mint tarragon is a good substitute when heat and humidity stunt French tarragon.

Features: foliage **Height:** 18–36"
Spread: 12–18" **Hardiness:** zones 3–8

Lady's Mantle
Alchemilla

Lady's mantle is a pretty carry over from the monastery garden of the Middle Ages. Perhaps better known as a popular perennial, lady's mantle is also a welcome addition to the herb garden as an edible and medicinal plant.

Growing

Lady's mantle grows well in **light shade** or **partial shade** with protection from the afternoon sun. Hot locations and excessive sun will scorch the leaves. The soil should be **fertile, humus rich, moist** and **well drained**.

The leaves can be sheared back in summer if they begin to look tired and heat stressed. New leaves will emerge. Spent flowers can be removed to reduce self-seeding, but any new plants are usually welcome.

Tips

Lady's mantle is a lovely plant to group under trees and along pathways. It can also be grown in containers. The young leaves can be used in salads or chopped and mixed into tzatziki or other yogurt- or sour cream-based dips.

Recommended

A. mollis (common lady's mantle) forms a mound of soft, rounded foliage and produces sprays of frothy-looking, yellowish green flowers in early summer.

Its airy blooms dry well for wreaths.

A. mollis (above & below)

Features: attractive, edible foliage; yellow or yellow-green, summer and early-fall flowers
Height: 8–18" **Spread:** 20–24"
Hardiness: zones 3–7

Lavender

Lavandula

L. angustifolia (above & below)

Lavender is considered the queen of herbs. A plant of ancient cultivation, this timeless herb traveled with the Romans, who bathed in its aromatic blooms. The clean scent and pretty color make it a valuable addition to any garden.

Growing

Lavenders grow best in **full sun**. The soil should be **average to fertile, alkaline** and very **well drained**. Once established, these plants are heat and drought tolerant. Plants can be sheared back in spring or after flowering.

Tips

Lavenders are wonderful, aromatic and sweet-smelling edging plants and can be trimmed to form the low hedges of a traditional herbal knot garden. They can be grown on patios in large urns and pots where the fabulous fragrance will be close at hand. Remember that the tap root needs room to burrow.

Recommended

L. angustifolia (English lavender) is a bushy, fragrant plant. It bears spikes of light purple flowers from mid-summer to fall. Continual picking encourages more and more blooms. The many cultivars include plants with white, pink or green flowers, silvery gray to olive green foliage and dwarf or compact habits. (Zones 5–8)

L. stoechas (French lavender) is a bushy, evergreen perennial with light green to gray-green, fringe-edged foliage. Tufts of light purple bracts top spikes of dark purple flowers. This type is best grown on a patio so that it can be taken indoors to a sunny window for winter. (Zones 8–9)

Features: fragrant, mid-summer and fall flowers in purple, pink, blue or white; fragrant, evergreen foliage; bushy habit **Height:** 8–36" **Spread:** 1–4' **Hardiness:** zones 5–9

Mexican Mint Tarragon

Tagetes

T. lucida

The fresh or dried leaves and flowers of this anise-scented plant are used to make a popular tea in Latin America and make a wonderful substitute for tarragon. Its pretty fall blooms are edible and decorative.

Growing

Mexican mint tarragon grows best in **full sun**. The soil should be of **average fertility** and **well drained**. Although these plants are fairly drought tolerant, they will perform best if watered regularly during dry spells.

Tips

Dot these plants here and there throughout your beds and borders for a pretty display as well as to take advantage of their reputed nematode-repelling properties. In New Jersey, they may also be grown in a large pot on a deck and taken inside for winter.

Recommended

T. lucida is a bushy, upright plant with narrow, toothy, dark green leaves. It bears bright yellow flowers in late summer and fall.

This plant has many culinary and medicinal properties and is even reputed to be hallucinogenic when specifically prepared. It is also used to treat scorpion bites and to remove ticks.

Also called: sweet mace, Texas tarragon
Features: attractive, fragrant foliage; bright yellow, fall flowers; drought tolerant
Height: 12–32" **Spread:** 8–18"
Hardiness: tender perennial grown as an annual

Mint

Mentha

M. x *piperita* 'Chocolate' (above)
M. x *piperita citrata* (below)

A few sprigs of fresh mint added to a pitcher of iced tea give it an added zip.

The cool, refreshing flavor of mint lends itself to tea and other hot or cold beverages. Mint sauce, made from freshly chopped leaves, is often served with lamb.

Growing

Mint grows well in **full sun** or **partial shade**. The soil should be **average to fertile, humus rich** and **moist**. These plants spread vigorously by rhizomes and may need a barrier in the soil to restrict their spread.

Tips

Mint is a good groundcover for damp spots. It grows well along ditches that may be periodically wet. It can also be used in beds and borders, but it may overwhelm less-vigorous plants. Use its vigorous habit to your advantage by planting mint under trees and in waste areas to suppress weed growth.

The flowers attract bees, butterflies and other pollinators to the garden. They can be picked and dried to use in wreaths and arrangements.

Recommended

There are many species, hybrids and cultivars of mint. *M.* x *piperita* (peppermint), *M.* x *piperita citrata* (orange mint, eau de cologne mint) and *M. spicata* (spearmint) are three of the most commonly grown culinary varieties. There are also more decorative varieties with variegated or curly leaves as well as varieties with unusual fruit-scented leaves.

Features: fragrant foliage; purple, pink or white, summer flowers **Height:** 6–36"
Spread: 36" or more **Hardiness:** zones 4–8

Oregano • Marjoram

Origanum

Oregano and marjoram are two of the best-known and most frequently used herbs. They are popular in stuffings, soups and stews, and no pizza is complete until it has been sprinkled with fresh or dried oregano leaves.

Growing

Oregano and marjoram grow best in **full sun**. The soil should be of **poor to average fertility, neutral to alkaline** and **well drained**. Marjoram prefers to be in moist, well-drained soil whereas oregano prefers drier conditions. The flowers attract pollinators to the garden.

Tips

Not all oreganos and marjorams are hardy in New Jersey. These perennials make a lovely addition to any border.

Recommended

O. majorana var. *hortensis* (marjoram) is upright and shrubby with light green, hairy leaves. It bears white or pink flowers in summer and can be grown as an annual where it is not hardy.

O. vulgare var. *hirtum* (oregano, Greek oregano) is the most flavorful culinary variety of oregano. The low, bushy plant has hairy, gray-green leaves and bears white flowers. Many other interesting varieties of *O. vulgare* are available, including those with golden, variegated or curly leaves.

In Greek, oros means "mountain" and ganos means "joy" or "beauty."

O. vulgare 'Aureum' (above & below)

Features: fragrant foliage; white or pink, summer flowers; bushy habit **Height:** 12–32"
Spread: 8–18" **Hardiness:** zones 5–9

Parsley
Petroselinum

P. crispum (above), *P. crispum* var. *crispum* (below)

Although usually used as a garnish, parsley is rich in vitamins and minerals and is reputed to freshen the breath after garlic- or onion-rich foods are eaten.

Growing

Parsley grows well in **full sun** or **partial shade**. The soil should be of **average to rich fertility, humus rich, moist** and **well drained**. Sow seeds directly in the garden or purchase flats of plants in market pots because parsley resents transplanting. If you start seeds early, use peat pots so the plants can be planted out without disruption.

Tips

Containers of parsley can be kept close to the house for easy picking. The bright green leaves and compact growth habit make parsley a good edging plant for beds and borders.

Recommended

P. crispum forms a clump of bright green, divided leaves. This plant is a biennial but is usually grown as an annual because it is the leaves that are desired, not the flowers or seeds. Cultivars may have flat or curly leaves. Flat leaves are more flavorful and curly are more decorative. Dwarf cultivars are also available.

Sprinkle chopped parsley on soups before serving and add a generous amount to boiled potatoes along with chives, dill and butter. Parsley also makes a tasty and nutritious addition to salads.

Features: attractive foliage **Height:** 8–24"
Spread: 12–24" **Hardiness:** zones 5–8;
grown as an annual

Rosemary
Rosmarinus

This fragrant little shrub is ancient and mystical in its timeless beauty and scent. The needle-like leaves are used to flavor a wide variety of foods including chicken, pork, lamb, rice, tomato and eggs.

Growing
Rosemary prefers **full sun** but tolerates partial shade. The soil should be of **poor to average fertility** and **well drained**. These tender shrubs may make it through winter if they are planted in a protected place near the foundation of a home; otherwise they must be moved indoors in winter.

Tips
Rosemary can be grown in a shrub border in most New Jersey gardens, but it might not return in spring. It can be grown as a container specimen and overwintered indoors. Low-growing, spreading plants can be included in a rock garden, along the top of a retaining wall or in hanging baskets.

Recommended
R. officinalis is a dense, bushy, evergreen shrub with narrow, dark green leaves. The habit varies somewhat between cultivars from strongly upright to prostrate and spreading. Flowers are usually in shades of blue, but pink-flowered cultivars are available. Plants generally bloom during cool weather and occasionally at other times. Cultivars are available that can survive in zone 6 in a sheltered location with winter protection. Plants rarely reach their mature size when grown in containers.

R. officinalis (above & below)

Place rosemary in a sunny window for winter. Water well, but allow it to dry out slightly between waterings.

Features: fragrant, evergreen foliage; bright blue, sometimes pink flowers **Height:** 8"–4'
Spread: 1–4' **Hardiness:** zones 8–10

Sage
Salvia

S. officinalis 'Icterina' (above)
S. officinalis 'Purpurea' (below)

Sage has been used since at least ancient Greek times as a medicinal and culinary herb and continues to be widely used for both those purposes today.

Culinary sage is perhaps best known as a flavoring for stuffing, but it has a great range of uses, including in soups, stews, sausages and dumplings.

Growing

Sage prefers **full sun** but tolerates light shade. The soil should be of **average fertility** and **well drained**. These plants benefit from a light mulch of compost each year. They are drought tolerant once established.

Tips

Sage is an attractive plant for the border, adding volume to the middle or as an attractive edging or feature plant near the front. Sage can also be grown in mixed planters.

Recommended

S. officinalis is a woody, mounding plant with soft, gray-green leaves. Spikes of light purple flowers appear in early and mid-summer. Many cultivars with attractive foliage are available, including the silver-leaved **'Berggarten,'** the purple-leaved **'Purpurea,'** the yellow-margined **'Icterina'** and the purple, green and cream variegated **'Tricolor,'** which has a pink flush to the new growth.

Features: fragrant, decorative foliage; blue or purple, summer flowers **Height:** 12–24" **Spread:** 18–36" **Hardiness:** zones 5–8

Sweet Cicely
Myrrhis

M. odorata (both photos)

Sweet cicely has a surprising variety of culinary uses, as the leaves, seeds and roots are all edible. It is also a very pretty shade plant.

Growing
Sweet cicely grows best in **partial shade** or **light shade** but tolerates full sun in a sufficiently moist soil. The soil should be of **average fertility, moist** and **well drained**. Plants self-seed, but not invasively.

Tips
This beautiful plant deserves to be included in shade gardens and borders and herb gardens. If plants begin to look tattered in mid-summer, they can be cut back, and fresh new growth will quickly emerge. If it is extremely hot, they might disappear until the following year.

Recommended
M. odorata forms a clump of soft, fragrant, fern-like leaves. It bears airy clusters of tiny, white flowers in spring.

Sweet cicely leaves are an excellent sugar replacement. They can be chopped and added to salads or mixed into yogurt. A handful of leaves added to stewed rhubarb will reduce the need for sugar by half. The roots can be cooked or roasted like parsnips. The seeds can be crushed and added to pies and other fruity dishes.

Features: fragrant, edible leaves, roots and seeds; white, spring flowers **Height:** 1–4'
Spread: 2–4' **Hardiness:** zones 3–8

Thyme

Thymus

T. vulgaris (above), *T. x citriodorus* (below)

Thyme is a popular culinary herb used in soups, stews and casseroles and with roasts. It is also a bathing, cleaning and medicinal herb.

Growing

Thyme prefers **full sun**. The soil should be **neutral to alkaline** and of **poor to average fertility**. Good drainage is essential. It is beneficial to work leaf mould and sharp limestone gravel into the soil to improve structure and drainage.

Tips

Thyme is useful for sunny, dry locations at the front of borders, between or beside paving stones, on rock gardens and rock walls and in containers on a porch or indoors. Once the plants have finished flowering, shear them back by about half to encourage new growth and to prevent the plants from becoming too woody.

Recommended

T. x citriodorus (lemon-scented thyme) forms a mound of lemon-scented, dark green foliage. The flowers are pale pink. Cultivars with silver- or gold-margined leaves are available.

T. vulgaris (common thyme) forms a bushy mound of dark green leaves. The flowers may be purple, pink or white. Cultivars with variegated leaves are available.

Features: bushy habit; fragrant, decorative foliage; purple, pink or white flowers
Height: 8–16" **Spread:** 8–16"
Hardiness: zones 4–9

Ajuga
Ajuga

A. reptans 'Caitlin's Giant' (above & below)

Nothing is prettier in spring than a purple carpet of ajuga planted along a woodland path in a shady garden.

Growing

Ajugas develop the best leaf color in **partial shade** or **light shade** but tolerate full shade. Excessive sun may scorch the leaves. Any **well-drained** soil is suitable. Divide these vigorous plants any time during the growing season.

When growing hybrids with fancy leaf coloration, remove any new growth or seedlings that revert to green.

Tips

Ajugas make excellent groundcovers for difficult sites such as exposed slopes and dense shade. They are also attractive in shrub borders, where their dense growth prevents the spread of all but the most tenacious weeds.

Recommended

A. genevensis (Geneva bugleweed) is a an upright, non-invasive species that bears blue, white or pink, spring flowers.

A. pyramidalis 'Metallica Crispa' (upright bugleweed) is a very slow-growing plant with bronzy, crinkly foliage and violet blue flowers.

A. reptans (common ajuga) is a low, quick-spreading groundcover. The many cultivars are grown for their colorful, often variegated foliage.

Also called: bugleweed **Features:** purple, pink, bronze, green, white or variegated foliage; late-spring to early-summer flowers in purple, blue, pink or white **Height:** 3–12"
Spread: 6–36" **Hardiness:** zones 3–8

Artemisia

Artemisia

A. *ludoviciana* 'Silver Queen' (above)
A. *ludoviciana* 'Valerie Finnis' (below)

Most of the artemisias are valued for their silvery foliage, not their flowers. Silver king has long been used in dried herbal wreaths and arrangements.

Growing

Artemisias grow best in **full sun**. The soil should be of **poor to average fertility** and **well drained**. These plants dislike wet, humid conditions.

When artemisias begin to look straggly, cut them back hard to encourage new growth and to maintain a neater form. Divide them every year or two when plant clumps appear to be thinning in the centers.

Tips

Use artemisias in rock gardens and borders. Their silvery gray foliage makes them good backdrop plants for brightly colored flowers. They are also useful for filling in spaces between other plants. Smaller forms may be used to create knot gardens. These plants can become invasive.

Recommended

A. ludoviciana 'Silver King' (silver king artemisia) is a compact plant with attractive, silvery foliage. This rapid spreader may be a bit too vigorous for some, but it is appreciated for crafts and makes a wonderful base for wreaths.

A. x 'Powis Castle' is a compact, mounding, shrubby plant with feathery, silvery gray foliage. This hybrid is reliably hardy to zone 6, but it can also grow in colder regions if planted with winter protection in a sheltered site.

A. schmidtiana (silvermound artemisia) is a low, dense, mound-forming perennial with feathery, hairy, silvery gray foliage. 'Nana' (dwarf silvermound) is very compact and grows only half the size of the species. (Zones 4–8)

Also called: wormwood, sage
Features: silvery gray, feathery or deeply lobed foliage **Height:** 6"–6' **Spread:** 12–36"
Hardiness: zones 3–8

Coleus
Solenostemon (Coleus)

*T*here is a coleus for everyone. From brash yellows, oranges and reds to deep maroon and rose selections, the colors, textures and variations are almost limitless. This plant is among the best for containers in the shade.

Growing
Coleus prefers to grow in **light shade** or **partial shade**, but it tolerates full shade if the shade isn't too dense and full sun if the plants are watered regularly. The soil should be of **average to rich fertility, humus rich, moist** and **well drained**.

Place the seeds in a refrigerator for one or two days to break their dormancy, then plant them on the soil surface because they need light to germinate. Seedlings will be green at first, but leaf variegation will develop as the plants mature. When flower buds develop, it is best to pinch them off because the plants tend to stretch out and become less attractive after they flower.

Tips
The bold, colorful foliage makes coleus dramatic when the plants are grouped together as edging plants or in beds, borders or mixed containers. Coleus can also be grown indoors as a houseplant in a bright room. Take cuttings in late summer and enjoy them all winter on your windowsills. In spring, move them back to the garden after the last frost date.

S. scutellarioides mixed cultivar (above & below)

Recommended
S. scutellarioides *(Coleus blumei* var. *verschaffeltii)* forms a bushy mound of foliage. The leaf edges range from slightly toothed to very ruffled. The leaves are usually multi-colored, with shades ranging from pale greenish yellow to deep purple-black. Dozens of cultivars are available, but many cannot be started from seed.

Features: brightly colored foliage; light purple flowers **Height:** 6–36" **Spread:** usually equal to height **Hardiness:** tender perennial grown as an annual

Dead Nettle

Lamium

L. maculatum 'White Nancy' and 'Purple Dragon' (above), *L. maculatum* 'Beacon Silver' (below)

These attractive plants, with their striped, dotted or banded, silver and green foliage, thrive on only the barest necessities of life.

Growing

Dead nettles prefer **partial to light shade**. They tolerate full sun but may become leggy. The soil should be of **average fertility, humus rich, moist** and **well drained**. The more fertile the soil, the more vigorously the plants will grow. These plants are drought tolerant when grown in the shade but can develop bare patches if allowed to dry out for extended periods. Divide and replant in fall if bare spots become unsightly.

Dead nettles remain more compact if sheared back after flowering. If they remain green over winter, shear them back in early spring.

Tips

These plants make useful groundcovers for woodland or shade gardens. They also work well under shrubs in a border, where the dead nettles will help keep weeds down. These plants can spread and become invasive in a wildflower garden.

Recommended

L. galeobdolon (*Lamiastrum galeobdolon;* yellow archangel) can be quite invasive, though the cultivars are less so. The flowers are yellow and bloom in spring to early summer. Several cultivars are available.

L. maculatum (spotted dead nettle) is the most commonly grown dead nettle. This low-growing, spreading species has green leaves with white or silvery markings and bears white, pink or mauve flowers. Many cultivars are available.

Also called: spotted dead nettle, lamium, yellow archangel **Features:** spring or summer flowers in white, pink, yellow or mauve; decorative, often variegated foliage **Height:** 4–24" **Spread:** indefinite **Hardiness:** zones 3–8

Dusty Miller

Senecio

S. cineraria 'Cirrus' (above), *S. cineraria* (below)

Dusty miller makes an artful addition to planters, window boxes and mixed borders where the soft, silvery gray, deeply lobed foliage makes a good backdrop to show off the brightly colored flowers of other annuals.

Growing

Dusty miller prefers **full sun** but tolerates light shade. The soil should be of **average fertility** and **well drained**.

Tips

The soft, silvery, lacy leaves of this plant are its main feature. Dusty miller is used primarily as an edging plant but also in beds, borders and containers.

Pinch off the flowers before they bloom. They aren't showy, and they steal energy that would otherwise go to producing more foliage.

Recommended

S. cineraria forms a mound of fuzzy, silvery gray, lobed or finely divided foliage. Many cultivars have been developed with impressive variations in the shade and shape of the foliage.

Mix dusty miller with geraniums and begonias to bring out the vibrant colors of those flowers.

Features: silvery foliage; neat habit
Height: 12–24" **Spread:** equal to or slightly less than height **Hardiness:** tender perennial grown as an annual

Euphorbia
Euphorbia

E. amygdaloides var. *robbiae* (above)
E. dulcis 'Chameleon' (right)

Euphorbias are excellent drought-tolerant plants; try them in the driest spot in your garden, and you won't be disappointed with the results.

Growing

Euphorbias grow well in **full sun** or **light shade**, and *E. a.* var. *robbiae* will also thrive in deep shade. The soil should be of **average fertility, moist, humus rich** and **well drained**. These plants are drought tolerant and can be invasive in a too-fertile soil. They do not tolerate wet conditions. Avoid dividing these plants, as they resent having their roots disturbed.

Tips

Use euphorbia in a mixed or herbaceous border, rock garden or lightly shaded border. If you group several together, they make an excellent groundcover for a dry, difficult-to-mow slope.

Recommended

E. amygdaloides var. *robbiae* (*E. robbiae*) is an evergreen with shiny, leathery, dark green leaves. It is a good choice in dry shade. It bears lime green flowers in spring and early summer. It spreads by runners and can be somewhat invasive if not kept in check.

E. dulcis is a compact, upright, mound-forming plant. The spring flowers and bracts are yellow-green. The dark bronzy green leaves turn red and orange in fall. 'Chameleon' has purple-red foliage that turns darker purple in fall. It bears clusters of chartreuse flowers.

Also called: spurge **Features:** bronzy green or red-purple foliage; yellow-bracted, chartreuse flowers **Height:** 12" **Spread:** 12" **Hardiness:** zones 4–9

Fescue

Festuca

This fine-leaved ornamental grass forms tufted clumps that resemble pin cushions. Its metallic blue coloring adds an all-season cooling accent to the garden.

Growing

Fescue thrives in **full sun to light shade**. The soil should be of **average fertility, moist** and **well drained**. Plants are drought tolerant once established. Fescue emerges early in the spring, so shear it back to 1" above the crown in late winter before new growth emerges. Shear off flower stalks just above the foliage to keep the plant tidy and to prevent self-seeding.

Tips

With its fine texture and distinct blue color, this grass can be used as a single specimen in a rock garden or container planting. Plant fescue in drifts to create a sea of blue or a handsome edge to a bed, border or pathway. It looks attractive in both formal and informal gardens. For a large sweep of blue, combine it with one of the taller blue grasses, or be daring and add a red grass or two.

Recommended

F. glauca (blue fescue) forms tidy, tufted clumps of fine, blue-toned foliage and panicles of flowers in May and June. Cultivars and hybrids come in varying heights and in shades ranging from bright blue to olive green. **'Elijah Blue,' 'Boulder Blue,' 'Skinner's Blue'** and **'Solling'** are popular selections.

F. glauca 'Elijah Blue' (above), *F. glauca* (below)

If you enjoy blue grass, you might also like the large, coarse-textured blue oat grass, Helicotrichon sempervirens *'Saphirsprudel' (Sapphire Fountain), which can reach 4' in height when in flower. It looks nice in the back of a border with fescue in front.*

Also called: blue fescue **Features:** blue to blue-green foliage; color that persists into winter; habit **Height:** 6–12" **Spread:** 10–12" **Hardiness:** zones 3–9

Licorice Plant

Helichrysum

H. petiolare 'Silver' (above), *H. petiolare* 'Limelight' (below)

The silvery sheen of licorice plant is caused by a fine, soft pubescence on the leaves. It is a perfect complement to any plant because silver is the ultimate blending color. It drapes nicely from pots of perennials, herbs or annuals.

Growing

Licorice plant prefers **full sun**. The soil should be of **poor to average fertility, neutral to alkaline** and **well drained**. Licorice plant wilts when the soil dries

Licorice plant is a good indicator plant for hanging baskets. When you see licorice plant wilting, it is time to water your baskets.

but revives quickly once watered. If it outgrows its space, snip it back with a pair of pruners, shears or even scissors.

Tips

Licorice plant is a perennial grown as an annual and is prized for its foliage rather than its flowers. Include it in your hanging baskets, planters and window boxes to provide a soft, silvery backdrop for the colorful flowers of other plants. Licorice plant can also be used as a groundcover in beds, borders and rock gardens and along the tops of retaining walls.

Recommended

H. petiolare is a trailing plant with fuzzy, gray-green leaves. Cultivars are more common than the species and include varieties with lime green, silver or variegated leaves.

Features: trailing habit; colorful, fuzzy foliage **Height:** 20" **Spread:** about 36"; sometimes up to 6' **Hardiness:** tender perennial grown as an annual

Liriope

Liriope

Liriope is a popular groundcover, almost impervious to drought, heat, humidity and most garden pests and diseases. Plant it with lots of spring-blooming bulbs to hide its sparse spring foliage; later it will camouflage their fading foliage.

Growing

Liriope grows best in **light shade** or **partial shade** but tolerates both full sun and full shade well. The soil should be of **average fertility, humus rich, acidic, moist** and **well drained**. Its evergreen leaves are prone to drying out in winter, so plant it in a sheltered location.

Cut back faded growth in late winter or early spring to make way for new growth and to keep plants looking tidy. An electric hand clipper or weed whacker can make the task of shearing off spent foliage less of a chore. For large expanses, use a lawnmower.

Tips

Liriope makes a fantastic dense groundcover, ideal for keeping weeds down in a variety of locations. Include it in beds, borders and woodland gardens, near water features or under trees where grass won't grow. It should not be planted with delicate perennials or annuals.

Recommended

L. muscari forms a mass of low clumps of strap-like, evergreen leaves. It bears spikes of purple flowers from late summer through fall. Cultivars are available.

L. muscari 'Peedee Ingot' (above)
L. muscari 'Variegata' (below)

These plants are heat-tolerant, making them popular where summer temperatures are frequently high and plants that stay green and attractive with minimal care are much appreciated.

Also called: lilyturf **Features:** clump-forming perennial with narrow, strap-like leaves; late-summer through mid-fall flowers in shades of purple and blue **Height:** 8–18" **Spread:** 18" **Hardiness:** zones 6–9

Lungwort
Pulmonaria

P. saccharata (above & below)

Lungworts have highly attractive foliage that ranges in color from apple green to silver-spotted and olive to dark emerald green. Most also have wonderful early-spring blooms.

Growing
Lungworts prefer **partial to full shade**. The soil should be **fertile, humus rich**, somewhat **moist** and very **well drained**. Rot can occur in very wet soil.

To keep lungworts tidy and show off the fabulous foliage, deadhead the plants by shearing them back lightly after flowering. Divide them in early summer after flowering or in fall. Provide the newly planted divisions with lots of water to help them re-establish.

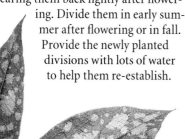

Tips
Lungworts make useful and attractive groundcovers for shady borders, woodland gardens and pond and stream edges.

Recommended
P. longifolia (long-leaved lungwort) forms a dense clump of long, narrow, white-spotted, green leaves and bears clusters of blue flowers.

P. officinalis (common lungwort, spotted dog) forms a loose clump of white-spotted, evergreen foliage. The flowers open pink and mature to blue. Cultivars are available.

P. saccharata (Bethlehem sage) forms a compact clump of large, white-spotted, evergreen leaves and purple, red or white flowers. Many cultivars are available.

Features: decorative, mottled foliage; blue, red, pink or white, spring flowers
Height: 8–24" **Spread:** 8–36"
Hardiness: zones 3–8

Maidenhair Fern

Adiantum

A. pedatum (above & below)

These charming, delicate-looking, native ferns add a graceful touch to a woodland planting. Their unique habit and texture will stand out in any garden.

Growing

Maidenhair ferns grow well in **light shade** or **partial shade** but tolerate full shade. The soil should be of **average fertility, humus rich, slightly acidic** and **moist**. These plants rarely need dividing, but they can be divided in spring to propagate more plants.

Tips

These lovely ferns will do well in any shaded spot in the garden. Include them in rock gardens, woodland gardens, shaded borders and beneath shade trees. They also make an attractive addition to a shaded planting next to a water feature or on a slope where the foliage can be seen when it sways in the breeze.

Recommended

A. pedatum forms a spreading mound of delicate, arching fronds. Light green leaflets stand out against the black stems, and the whole plant turns bright yellow in fall. Spores are produced on the undersides of the leaflets.

Try growing the fine-textured and delicate maidenhair fern with hostas and lungworts, and enjoy the lovely contrast in texture. It is also wonderful with native woodland wildflowers.

Also called: northern maidenhair
Features: deciduous, perennial fern; summer and fall foliage; habit **Height:** 12–24"
Spread: 12–24" **Hardiness:** zones 2–8

Miscanthus
Miscanthus

M. sinensis var. purpurescens (above)
M. sinensis 'Zebrinus' (below)

Miscanthus is one of the most popular and majestic of all the ornamental grasses. Its graceful foliage dances in the wind and makes an impressive sight all year long.

Growing

Miscanthus prefers **full sun**. The soil should be of **average fertility, moist** and **well drained**, though some selections tolerate wet soil. All selections are drought tolerant once established. Leave the foliage in place to provide winter interest, and then cut it back in spring before the new growth starts.

Tips

Give these magnificent beauties room to spread so you can fully appreciate their form. The plants' heights will determine the best place for each selection in the border. They create dramatic impact in groups or as seasonal screens.

Recommended

There are many cultivars of **M. sinensis**, all distinguished by the white midrib on the leaf blade. Some popular selections include **'Gracillimus'** (maiden grass), with long, fine-textured leaves; **'Grosse Fontaine'** (large fountain), a tall, wide-spreading, early-flowering selection; **'Morning Light'** (variegated maiden grass), a short, delicate plant with fine, white leaf edges; **var. *purpurescens*** (flame grass), with foliage that turns bright orange in early fall; **'Strictus'** (porcupine grass), a tall, stiff, upright selection with horizontal yellow bands on the leaves; and **'Zebrinus'** (zebra grass), an arching grass with horizontal yellow bands on the leaves.

Also called: eulalia, Japanese silver grass
Features: upright, arching habit; colorful summer and fall foliage; pink, copper or silver, late-summer and fall flowers; winter interest
Height: 4–8' **Spread:** 2–4'
Hardiness: zones 5–8

Ostrich Fern
Matteuccia

These popular ferns are revered for their delicious spring fronds and their stately, vase-shaped habit.

Growing

Ostrich ferns prefer **partial shade** or **light shade** but tolerate full shade and even full sun if the soil is kept moist. The soil should be **average to fertile, humus rich, neutral to acidic** and **moist**. The leaves may scorch if the soil is not moist enough. These ferns are aggressive spreaders that reproduce by spores. Unwanted plants can be pulled up and composted or given away.

Tips

These ferns appreciate a moist woodland garden and are often found growing wild alongside woodland streams and creeks. Useful in shaded borders, these plants are quick to spread, to the delight of those who enjoy the tightly curled, young fronds as a culinary delicacy.

Recommended

M. struthiopteris (*M. pennsylvanica*) forms a circular cluster of slightly arching, feathery fronds. Stiff, brown, fertile fronds, covered in reproductive spores, stick up in the center of the cluster in late summer and persist through winter. It is a popular choice for dried arrangements.

M. struthiopteris (above & below)

Ostrich ferns are grown commercially for their edible fiddleheads. The new spring fronds taste delicious lightly steamed and served with butter. Remove the bitter, reddish brown, papery coating before steaming.

Also called: fiddlehead fern
Features: perennial fern; foliage; habit
Height: 3–5' **Spread:** 12–36" or more
Hardiness: zones 1–8

Reed Grass
Calamagrostis

C. x acutiflora 'Avalanche' (above)
C. x acutiflora 'Karl Foerster' (below)

If you like how reed grass holds its flowers high above its mounded foliage, consider Deschampsia (tufted hair grass) and Molinia (moor grass) and their species and cultivars. Some have yellow-striped foliage.

This is a graceful, metamorphic grass that changes its habit and flower color throughout the seasons.

Growing

Reed grass grows best in **full sun**. The soil should be **fertile, moist** and **well drained**. Heavy clay and dry soils are tolerated. It may be susceptible to rust in cool, wet summers or in areas with poor air circulation. Rain and heavy snow may cause it to flop temporarily, but it quickly bounces back. Cut it back to 2–4" in very early spring before new growth begins. Divide it if it begins to die out in the center.

Tips

Whether it's used as a single stately focal point, in small groupings or in large drifts, this is a desirable, low-maintenance grass. It combines well with perennials that bloom in late summer and fall.

Recommended

C. x acutiflora **'Karl Foerster'** (Foerster's feather reed grass), the most popular selection, forms a loose mound of green foliage from which the airy, bottlebrush flowers emerge in June. The flowering stems have a loose, arching habit when they first emerge but grow more stiff and upright over summer. Other cultivars include **'Overdam,'** a compact, less-hardy selection with white leaf edges. Watch for a new introduction called **'Avalanche,'** which has a white center stripe.

Features: open habit becomes upright; silvery pink flowers turn rich tan; green foliage turns bright gold in fall; winter interest
Height: 3–5' **Spread:** 24–36"
Hardiness: zones 4–9

Sea Oats
Chasmanthium

This native grass is at home in moist, shady woodlands, but its bamboo-like foliage gives it a tropical flair.

Growing

Sea oats thrive in **full shade to full sun**, though they must stay moist in full sun to avoid leaf scorch. The upright, cascading habit relaxes in deep shade. The soil should be **fertile** and **moist**, but dry soils are tolerated.

Sea oats vigorously self-seed, but the seedlings are easily removed and composted or shared with friends. Divide to control the rapid spread. Cut this plant back each spring to 2" above the ground.

Tips

Sea oats are tremendous plants for moist, shady areas. When in full bloom, their upright to cascading habit makes an attractive planting alongside a stream or pond, in a large drift or in a container. These plants can become invasive in the garden when growing conditions are good.

Recommended

C. latifolium forms a spreading clump of unique, bright green, bamboo-like foliage that turns bronze in fall. The scaly, dangling spikelet flowers are arranged nicely on delicate stems just slightly above the foliage.

C. latifolium (above & below)

These dry nicely and look good in dried arrangements.

Also called: northern sea oats
Features: bamboo-like foliage; unusual flowers; winter interest **Height:** 32"–4'
Spread: 18–24" **Hardiness:** zones 5–9

Sedum
Sedum

S. *spurium* 'Dragon's Blood' (above), S. *acre* (right)

These low-growing, fast-spreading plants are drought tolerant, making them ideal for supressing weeds and filling in difficult areas.

Growing
Sedums prefer **full sun** but tolerate partial shade. The soil should be of **average fertility, neutral to alkaline** and very **well drained**. Too much fertilizer or water will result in weak, lanky plants. Divide in spring when needed.

The low, trailing species of sedum make interesting houseplants. Try growing two or three with a variety of colorfully leaved plants in a pot or hanging basket in a sunny window.

Tips
These low-growing sedums make wonderful groundcovers and additions to rock gardens and rock walls. They can also be used to edge beds and borders.

Recommended
S. acre (gold moss stonecrop) is a low-growing , wide-spreading plant that bears small, yellow-green flowers. It can spread aggressively. Cultivars are available and include silver variegated and yellow-leaved selections.

S. spurium (two-row stonecrop) forms a low, wide mat of foliage with deep pink or white flowers. Many cultivars are available and are often grown for their colorful foliage, including red-, bronze- and purple-leaved selections.

Also called: stonecrop **Features:** yellow, white, red or pink, summer to fall flowers; decorative, fleshy foliage **Height:** 2–4" **Spread:** 24" or more **Hardiness:** zones 3–9

Sensitive Fern

Onoclea

O. sensibilis (above & below)

Common along stream banks and in wooded areas in the Middle Atlantic States, this native fern thrives in moist and shaded conditions.

Growing

Sensitive ferns grow best in **light shade** but tolerate full shade and partial shade. The fronds can scorch if exposed to too much sun. The soil should be **fertile, humus rich** and **moist**, although some drought is tolerated. These plants are sensitive to frost and can be easily damaged by late and early frosts.

Tips

Sensitive ferns like to live in damp, shady places. Include them in shaded borders, woodland gardens and other locations with protection from the wind.

Recommended

O. sensibilis forms a mass of light green, deeply lobed, arching fronds. Fertile fronds are produced in late summer and persist through winter. The spores are produced in structures that look like black beads, which give the fertile fronds a decorative appearance that makes them a popular addition to floral arrangements.

Features: deciduous, perennial fern; attractive foliage; habit **Height:** 24"
Spread: indefinite **Hardiness:** zones 4–9

Sweet Potato Vine

Ipomoea

This vigorous, rambling annual with lime green, bruised purple or green, pink and cream variegated leaves can make any gardener look like a genius.

Growing

Grow sweet potato vine in **full sun**. Any type of soil will do, but a **light, well-drained** soil of **poor fertility** is preferred.

Tips

Sweet potato vine is a great addition to mixed planters, window boxes and hanging baskets. In a rock garden it will scramble about, and along the top of a retaining wall it will cascade over the edge. Although this plant is a vine, its bushy habit and colorful leaves make it more useful as a foliage plant.

Recommended

I. batatas (sweet potato vine) is a twining climber that is grown for its attractive foliage rather than its flowers. Several cultivars are available.

I. batatas 'Blackie' (above)
I. batatas 'Margarita' (below)

As a bonus when you pull up your plant at the end of summer, you can eat any tubers (sweet potatoes) that have formed, or store the tubers dry in a bin to plant the next year.

Features: decorative foliage **Height:** about 12" **Spread:** up to 10' **Hardiness:** annual

Sweet Woodruff

Galium

G. *odoratum* (above & below)

Sweet woodruff is a groundcover with abundant good qualities: attractive, light green foliage that smells like new-mown hay when dried; profuse white, spring flowers; and the ability to fill in garden spaces without taking over.

Growing

This plant prefers **partial shade**. It will grow well, but will not bloom well, in full shade. The soil should be **humus rich**, **slightly acidic** and evenly **moist**. Sweet woodruff competes well with other plant roots and does well where some other groundcovers, like vinca, fail to thrive.

Sweet woodruff's vanilla-scented dried leaves and flowers have been used to scent bed linens and potpourri.

Tips

Sweet woodruff makes a fast-spreading woodland groundcover. It forms a beautiful green carpet and loves the same conditions in which azaleas and rhododendrons thrive. Interplant it with spring-flowering bulbs for a fantastic display in spring.

Recommended

G. odoratum is a low, spreading groundcover. It bears clusters of star-shaped, white flowers in a flush in late spring, and these continue to appear sporadically through mid-summer.

Features: deciduous, perennial groundcover; white, late-spring to mid-summer flowers; fragrant foliage; habit **Height:** 12–18"
Spread: indefinite **Hardiness:** zones 3–8

Switch Grass
Panicum

P. virgatum cultivar (above)
P. virgatum 'Heavy Metal' (below)

ative to the prairie grasslands, switch grass naturalizes equally well in an informal border and a natural meadow.

Growing

Switch grass thrives in **full sun, light shade** or **partial shade**. The soil should be of **average fertility** and **well drained**, although plants adapt to both moist and dry soils and tolerate conditions ranging from heavy clay to lighter sandy soil. Cut it back to 2–4" from the ground in early spring. The flower stems may break under heavy, wet snow or in exposed, windy sites.

Tips

Plant switch grass singly in small gardens, in large groups in spacious borders or at the edges of ponds or pools for a dramatic, whimsical effect. The seed heads attract birds and the foliage changes color in fall, so place this plant where you can enjoy both features.

Recommended

P. virgatum (switch grass) is suited to wild meadow gardens. Some of its popular cultivars include **'Heavy Metal'** (blue switch grass), an upright plant with narrow, steely blue foliage flushed with gold and burgundy in fall; **'Prairie Sky'** (blue switch grass), an arching plant with deep blue foliage; and **'Shenandoah'** (red switch grass), with red-tinged green foliage that turns burgundy in fall.

Features: clumping habit; green, blue or burgundy foliage; airy panicles of flowers; fall color; winter interest **Height:** 3–5' **Spread:** 30–36" **Hardiness:** zones 3–9

Glossary

Acidic soil: soil with a pH lower than 7.0

Annual: a plant that germinates, flowers, sets seed and dies in one growing season

Alkaline soil: soil with a pH higher than 7.0

Basal foliage: leaves that form from the crown, at the base of the plant

Bract: a modified leaf at the base of a flower or flower cluster

Corm: a bulb-like, food-storing, underground stem, resembling a bulb without scales

Crown: the part of the plant at or just below soil level where the shoots join the roots

Cultivar: a cultivated plant variety with one or more distinct differences from the species, e.g., in flower color or disease resistance

Deadhead: to remove spent flowers to maintain a neat appearance and encourage a longer blooming season

Direct sow: to sow seeds directly in the garden

Dormancy: a period of plant inactivity, usually during winter or unfavorable conditions

Double flower: a flower with an unusually large number of petals

Espalier: a tree trained from a young age to grow on a single plane—often along a wall or fence

Genus: a category of biological classification between the species and family levels; the first word in a scientific name indicates the genus

Grafting: a type of propagation in which a stem or bud of one plant is joined onto the rootstock of another plant of a closely related species

Hardy: capable of surviving unfavorable conditions, such as frost, without protection

Hip: the fruit of a rose, containing the seeds

Humus: decomposed or decomposing organic material in the soil

Hybrid: a plant resulting from natural or human-induced cross-breeding between varieties, species or genera

Neutral soil: soil with a pH of 7.0

Offset: a horizontal branch that forms at the base of a plant and produces new plants from buds at its tips

Panicle: a compound flower structure with groups of flowers on short stalks

Perennial: a plant that takes three or more years to complete its life cycle

pH: a measure of acidity or alkalinity; the soil pH influences availability of nutrients for plants

Rhizome: a root-like, food-storing stem that grows horizontally at or just below soil level, from which new shoots may emerge

Rootball: the root mass and surrounding soil of a plant

Seedhead: dried, inedible fruit that contains seeds; the fruiting stage of the inflorescence

Self-seeding: reproducing by means of seeds without human assistance, so that new plants constantly replace those that die

Semi-double flower: a flower with petals in two or three rings

Single flower: a flower with a single ring of typically four or five petals

Species: the fundamental unit of biological classification; the entity from which cultivars and varieties are derived

Standard: a shrub or small tree grown with an erect main stem, accomplished either through pruning and training or by grafting the plant onto a tall, straight stock

Sucker: a shoot that comes up from the root, often some distance from the plant; it can be separated to form a new plant once it develops its own roots

Tender: incapable of surviving the climatic conditions of a given region and requiring protection from frost or cold

Tuber: the thick section of a rhizome bearing nodes and buds

Variegation: foliage that has more than one color, often patched or striped or bearing leaf margins of a different color

Variety: a naturally occurring variant of a species

Index of Recommended Plant Names

Main entries are in **boldface**; botanical names are in *italics*.

Author Biographies

Lorraine Kiefer, a professional horticulturist, writer and floral designer, has gardened all her life. She is founder and chairman of the South Jersey unit of the Herb Society of America and serves on the Horticulture Committee of the National Herb Garden in Washington, DC. Lorraine teaches herb and landscaping classes, both at Gloucester County College and at Triple Oaks Nursery and Herb Garden in Franklinville, New Jersey, the business she and her husband Ted started in the mid-1970s. She writes two weekly garden columns and also writes articles for garden journals and magazines. Some of Lorraine's articles and most of her classes may be seen on her website, <www.tripleoaks.com>.

Alison Beck has gardened since she was a child. She has a diploma in Horticulture and a Bachelor of Arts in Creative Writing. Alison has co-authored many best-selling gardening guides. Her books showcase her talent for practical advice and her passion for gardening.

Acknowledgments

I would like to acknowledge my family, who instilled in me a love of gardening so many, many years ago. I especially thank my grandmother, Stella Grochowski, who was my first gardening buddy, and my other grandmother, Frances Caccese, who had a wonderful garden to play in, too. I thank my parents, Lillian and Joseph Grochowski, who also loved plants and gardening and who inspired me to follow my dreams.

Of course I thank my constant gardening partner throughout the years, my husband Ted Kiefer, and our three sons, Ted, Joe and Eric, who all are consummate gardeners, as well as their wives Sharon and Lisa and our grandchildren Tanner, Olivia, Emma and Lilli, and all the rest of the family who come to walk in the gardens with me.

I thank Triple Oaks Nursery, where our many display gardens inspire me daily. And finally, I thank all the local editors who have helped and encouraged me so many times. —*Lorraine Kiefer*